Wine of Reunion

T0385577

Wine of Reunion
ARABIC POEMS OF RUMI

Translated and edited by
Nesreen Akhtarkhavari *and* **Anthony A. Lee**

Michigan State University Press | *East Lansing*

⊖ The paper used in this publication meets the minimum requirements
of ANSI/NISO Z39.48-1992 (R 1997) (Permanence of Paper).

Michigan State University Press
East Lansing, Michigan 48823-5245

Printed and bound in the United States of America.

26 25 24 23 22 21 20 19 18 17   1 2 3 4 5 6 7 8 9 10

LIBRARY OF CONGRESS CATALOGING-IN-PUBLICATION DATA
Names: Jalāl al-Dīn Rūmī, Maulana, 1207–1273. | Akhtarkhavari, Nesreen translator editor.
| Lee, Anthony A., 1947– translator editor.
Title: Wine of reunion : Arabic poems of Rumi / translated and edited by
Nesreen Akhtarkhavari and Anthony A. Lee.
Description: East Lansing : Michigan State University Press, 2017.
| Series: Arabic literature and language series | English translations of Arabic poems and
fragments, selected from Rumi's Divan-e Shams. | Includes bibliographical references.
Identifiers: LCCN 2016057887 | ISBN 9781611862638 (pbk. : alk. paper) | ISBN 9781609175450 (pdf)
| ISBN 9781628953145 (epub) | ISBN 9781628963144 (kindle)
Subjects: LCSH: Jalāl al-Dīn Rūmī, Maulana, 1207–1273—Translations into English.
Classification: LCC PK6480.E5 A45 2017 | DDC 891/.5511—dc23
LC record available at https://lccn.loc.gov/2016057887

Book design by Sharp Des!gns, East Lansing, Michigan
Cover design by Shaun Allshouse, www.shaunallshouse.com
Cover image is a detail of Jalal al-Din Rumi showing his love for his young disciple
Hussam al-Din Chelebi c. 1594. Extract from "Tardjomev-i-Thevakib,"
by the Mawlewiyya Dervich Aflaki Baghdad, the Pierpoint Morgan Library, New York.

Michigan State University Press is a member of the Green Press Initiative and is
committed to developing and encouraging ecologically responsible publishing
practices. For more information about the Green Press Initiative and the use
of recycled paper in book publishing, please visit *www.greenpressinitiative.org.*

Visit Michigan State University Press at *www.msupress.org*

CONTENTS

PREFACE

Mawlana Rumi (1207–1273) has been known to Western literary audiences for well over a century and has become almost a household name. The poems of this thirteenth-century Islamic teacher, scholar, and Sufi poet, whose full name was Muhammad Jalal al-Din al-Balkhi, have shaped Islamic consciousness for some eight hundred years. Translations of his poems can be found in many bookstores, and his life story is well known.

Rumi was born into a Muslim clerical family near the city of Balkh (in present-day northern Afghanistan) at the eastern edge of the Persian-speaking world. His family moved away from Balkh ahead of the Mongol invasion and wandered through Iran to Mecca. Rumi was taught by his father, Baha al-Din Walad, a Muslim scholar, theologian, and Sufi master. Upon the passing of his father, Shaykh Burhan al-Din Muhakkik Tirmidi, a scholar, Sufi mystic and former disciple of Rumi's father, became his mentor. He recognized and respected Rumi's intellectual and spiritual qualities and helped guide his learning.[1] Rumi went to study in Syria and then settled back in Konya, Anatolia (present-day Turkey), and, with the support of al-Tirmidi, he eventually began teaching and took over his father's position as the master of the Islamic school and the religious and spiritual leader of his congregation. Assuming the duties of the learned class, Rumi preached in the mosque, taught in advanced religious circles, and gathered a large number of students.

Rumi's focus changed when he met Shams e-Din Tabrizi,[2] a mystic Sufi master looking for a student worthy to teach the art of love. According to legend, when they met in the street, it was love at first sight. Shams, the wandering scholar, became Rumi's mystic partner, companion, spiritual guide, and teacher.[3] Rumi became so engrossed in his meditations and spiritual exercises with Shams that he abandoned his duties at the teaching circles and in the mosque to spend all of his time with his beloved Shams. This raised the resentment and envy of Rumi's students and companions.

Then, without any warning, Shams left the city of Konya and disappeared. Rumi was shocked and full of grief; he looked everywhere for his master. Although Shams returned to Konya briefly, he left for a second time and was never heard from again. Rumi was devastated, paralyzed with grief. For years, he searched for Shams, hoping to bring him back to Konya, but he never found him. In his inconsolable bereavement, Rumi poured out his thoughts and emotions in poetry, which became a vehicle for his love. In these poems, he tells about the agony that burned his soul.[4] Rumi finally found some peace in realizing that his love for Shams was still inside him, and he returned to his clerical and teaching duties.

Meanwhile, Rumi continued to explore this encompassing form of love in thousands of poems. He took new partners and found new spiritual companions, but he continued to express his love and dedication to Shams, whom he regarded the source of all inspiration. He believed that any other affection he had stemmed from his true love to Shams, a glimpse into the true love of the Divine.[5]

Rumi's major collection of ghazals and quatrains, known as *Divan-e Shams-e Tabrizi*,[6] is written mainly in Persian, but also includes some Arabic poems and a few poems with alternating Turkish and Persian, Greek and Persian hemstitches. The poems in the divan are of different types. The critical edition, based on the earliest manuscripts, contains 3,283 long poems (ghazals), 44 stanzaic poems (*tarji'at*), and 1,983 quatrains (rubaiyat). These include 90 long poems and 19 quatrains that are fully in Arabic.[7] Arabic can also be found as lines or as half-lines in many of the poems that are otherwise in Persian. Some are Arabic except for a final line in Persian. Many have a number of lines in Arabic within the body, with Persian verses preceding and following them. The Arabic lines in these poems are consistently self-contained and form coherent poems by themselves, without reference to the Persian sections of the full poem. The Arabic lines, in many cases, are constructed as quatrains, even when presented instead in the form of a classical qasida.[8] This is an interesting feature in some of the Arabic poems of Rumi that we believe merits further investigation.

Any reader of the poems in Rumi's divan will immediately realize that, in the Persian and the Arabic alike, Rumi is intoxicated by the wine of love, and yearns for reunion with his beloved. Love is the single subject of his discourse and the focus of his every composition. In these poems, Rumi invokes his own all-consuming, burning, and tragic love for Shams, his teacher, his friend, his mystic guide, and his lost lover. This love and quest are manifested in his poems as a divine love and a quest of reunion with the beloved. Rumi declares this love as the purpose of his life and the only path to salvation.

Part of a Wider Sufi Movement

It is important to note that Rumi's work is not an isolated phenomenon. His poems, images, books, and the concepts they introduce are part of a larger volume of Sufi tradition written by Arab and Persian scholars, philosophers, and poets. This movement started in Basra and Kufa in Iraq as early as the second century after the Prophet Muhammad (570–632). The first adherents to the Sufi tradition were devoted Muslims who zealously guarded piety and renounced pleasure, wealth, and power. Influenced by Greek philosophy and the practices of Christian monks, they abandoned society to lead a secluded life devoted to service that they believed would bring them closer to God. They saw themselves as following in the footsteps of the early companions of the Prophet.

This ascetic movement further evolved during the Umayyad period (661–750), led by scholars such as Hasan al-Basri (642–728); his teachings shaped the early philosophy that sustained the movement. Rabi'a al-'Adawiyya (713–801), a younger woman who was a contemporary of al-Basri, a mystic poet also from Basra, was the first to introduce the concept of intimacy with God and employ poetry with physical and erotic images to describe this Divine Love. Rabi'a lived in abject poverty, was sold into slavery, and then she turned to a life of worship and piety. This impressed her master who finally set her free. Through her spontaneous erotic verses, she praised her beloved God and expressed her love and devotion to him. She believed that people should worship God not to secure favor or for fear of punishment but for God's own sake and for love of his eternal beauty.

Sufi thought continued to evolve to include the complete denouncement of the material world and absolute devotion to God, as a slave is to a master. This was especially advocated by Ibrahim ibn Adham, a wealthy prince from Balk (d. 782) who believed that solitary striving was the way to attain God's presence. The doctrine of these early Sufis became the ground upon which the advanced theology of Sufism was eventually built.

With the start of the Abbasid period (750), a Sufi ideology embedded in mystical practices and that advocated following a fixed spiritual path in the quest for a personal vision of God developed through the work of scholars who contributed significantly to the establishment, articulation, and recognition of Sufi doctrines and practices.[9] This alternative expression of faith was considered by many as a deviation from orthodox Islamic doctrine. This led to widespread condemnation and a wave of brutal persecution. One of the most influential figures of this period was Husayn ibn-Mansur al-Hallaj, a passionate exponent of Divine Love. Through poetry, he openly proclaimed union with God in the streets of Baghdad, raising the anger of religious scholars and ordinary people alike. Eventually, al-Hallaj was accused of blasphemy and was executed. His beautiful mystical Arabic poetry complements the work of Rabi'a al-'Adawiyya, establishing many of the images and concepts that Sufi poets have used throughout the ages.

Another Sufi scholar and poet of this period was Abu-Hamid Muhammad al-Ghazali—arguably one of the most prolific writers and influential scholars of his time. His theological and philosophical scholarship, coupled with his ability to argue and lucidly present his views, were critical in popularizing Sufism and placing it more in line with mainstream Islam in certain regions.

Sufi manuals and treatises started to appear in the tenth century as part of the trend to write textbooks for all branches of natural and social sciences. The Sufi manuals were, for the most part, written and published by Sufis themselves.[10] They recounted in detail Sufi philosophy, spiritual practices, and biographies of the saints. At the same time these manuals were published, poetic works, mostly in Persian, written by a series of Sufi masters and poets such as Omar Khayyam, Sana'i, 'Attar, and Rumi,[11] gained popularity. These poets, with their new, distinctive uses of language and vivid imagery, expanded the basic Sufi concepts and expressions.[12]

Another Sufi master of the time was Arab Andalusian Muslim scholar, philosopher, and poet Ibn Arabi.[13] Ibn Arabi was born in Spain in 1165, lived much of his life in Syria, and died in Damascus in 1240. He was another one of the most prolific writers, distinguished scholars, and inspirational poets. Sufis regard him as the greatest master and a genuine saint. Even though Rumi knew some of Ibn Arabi's disciples and was familiar with his writings, whether he was influenced by his doctrine or not is controversial.[14]

As mentioned earlier, Rumi was a Muslim scholar and teacher who mastered the Islamic sciences, as had his father, Baha al-Din Walad, also known the Sultan of the scholars, who had his own school and followers. The Sufi tradition at the time promoted the need for a master to guide the learner in the path of God. After the passing of his father, Rumi became the disciple of Shaykh Burhan al-Din Muhakkik Tirmidi, a distinguished disciple of his late father. At his teacher's recommendation, Rumi went to Aleppo and Damascus to further his studies. On the way back, Rumi visited Shaykh Burhan al-Din in Kayseri, where he completed a "forty-day initiation that resulted in a full-fledged acceptance into the Sufi path."[15] Rumi was respected by the people and rulers of the region, and by contemporary scholars. He had the good fortune to meet a number of renowned Sufi masters and poets from an early age and was influenced by some, especially Sana'i and 'Attar.

In addition to mastering Persian, Rumi's first language and the language of poetry and literature in the region, he studied Arabic, which was required for teaching and Islamic scholarship. As mentioned earlier, he frequently traveled to Syria, the Arab centers of learning at the time. Further, Rumi loved Arabic poetry, especially the work of Abu at-Tayyib al-Mutanabbi (d. 965), which influenced the form and rhyme of many of his Arabic poems.[16]

The greatest contribution of the Sufis, including the work of Rumi, has been a vision of Islam free of hatred, the desire for revenge, and the urge to violence. An Islam based on love, compassion, charity, service, mystic vision, and a personal relationship with God. It is what launched Rumi into global prominence in modern times and allowed his work to transcend the limitations of time and place.

This Volume

Wine of Reunion contains translations of some of Rumi's Arabic verses from *Divan Shams-e Tabrizi.*[17] This volume contains poems that have not been published in English before, extending access to his rarely translated Arabic poems, which are as direct, intense, and erotic as his Persian poems.

Nesreen Akhtarkhavari, carefully reviewed the Arabic poems in collaboration with Aref Awad al-Helal, a Jordanian poet and linguist. A small number of corrections were made to apply conventional spellings, incorporate accurate diacritical marks and word endings, and revise grammatical or spelling errors. This makes the book a valuable addition to the current literature available to Arabic and English readers and scholars interested in Rumi's work.

Following English literary convention, the Arabic and English poems in this volume have been given titles, which were not in the originals. The poems have been grouped together into five parts, organized around different themes. You Are Beautiful! includes poems devoted to Rumi's love and adoration for Shams. For example, in "Kill Me Now" Rumi writes:

> Master! You're my Teacher, and you're my Strength,
> my Guide, my Savior in calamity.
> More, you are my shelter, my protection,
> my eternal life—all that I can be.

The poems in The Agony of Love explore every aspect of the forlorn lover's journey, from fascination and seduction to ecstatic union to bitter disappointment and loss. Love brings pain. Rumi mourns the loss of his beloved Shams as a spiritual journey. Rumi, like other Sufis, believes that the lover must endure hardship to reach his goal. In one heartbreaking passage from "The Agony of Love," Rumi calls to Shams:

> You say I should use patience as my balm?
> No, don't think that my love can be that calm.
> I couldn't stand your loss for one moment
> if I didn't think you'd return each dawn.

Rumi's language of love, at least in Arabic, is highly erotic, as well as deeply spiritual. The language of spirituality and the language of sexuality are so intertwined and blended that they are inseparable. As in all Arab cultures, Rumi does not understand sex to be a barrier to spiritual enlightenment. Quite the opposite, as can be seen in "The Path of Love":

> The best of life is on the path of love:
> a black-eyed maiden's wink, consent to meet.
> I don't find her on some deserted street
> but in gardens with others just as sweet.

The metaphors are chosen carefully and are deliberately ambiguous. In "My Heart Melts," Rumi expresses his longing for a young man, and describes him physically, combining the best of what different cultures offer:

> You are so young, and your body so fresh.
> Not far from days when you were drinking milk.
> A princely face, and Turkish from behind,
> Daylam hair, a chin like Romans carry.[18]

Rumi lived in the world of medieval Islam. His society freely accepted a premodern understanding of desire that differs from our own. The sexuality of centuries past was less compartmentalized, less differentiated, less medicalized than it is in our own time. Rumi far predates our modern notions of homosexuality and heterosexuality, relying on early Arab and Persian traditions that was more tolerant to same-gender relationships and intimacy within the boundaries of their cultural context.

The reader may be reminded of William Shakespeare's sonnet 20, written to a young man with whom the bard had become passionately fascinated:

> A woman's face with Nature's own hand painted
> Hast thou, the master-mistress of my passion;
> A woman's gentle heart, but not acquainted

With shifting change as is false women's fashion;
An eye more bright than theirs, less false in rolling,
Gilding the object whereupon it gazeth;
A man in hue, all hues in his controlling.

So, we are not entirely in uncharted territory when we read Rumi's poem. Nor was it uncommon for Rumi to express a full-bodied, intimate love in poems when addressing Shams-e Tabrizi, the hospitable wine bearer (always a young man) of Sufi imagery, or the beautiful virgins (houri) of heaven. The intensity of this love can be startling but also instructive. It is all part of the lover's journey toward the divine.

To a certain extent, of course, same-sex love is suggested by all expressions of devotion to God when God is conceived of as male and the devotee is a man. There are famous examples of this in Christian mystical poetry as well. John Donne, for example, addressed Christ with his Holy Sonnet 14:

Take me to you, imprison me, for I
Except you enthrall me, never shall be free,
Nor ever chaste, except you ravish me.

Franklin Lewis has argued in his exhaustive book on Rumi that the norms of masculinity of the time would have precluded any sexual relationship between Shams and Rumi.[19] Many of Rumi's poems clearly express homoerotic themes. However, these should be understood, alongside the other tropes and metaphors used in his poems—death, madness, seduction, fire, drunkenness—as attempts to capture a spiritual ecstasy that is beyond description. On this quest, nothing is taboo. He will use any means to get us to Divine Love through poetry and rhyme, including an idealized expression of homoerotic desire and full descriptions of the agony of lost love.

The poems in Wine of Reunion explore another one of these transgressive Sufi metaphors. Wine is strictly forbidden in Islam, but Rumi, like other Sufi poets before him, exalts wine as the elixir of life and the only path to enlightenment.[20] Wine signifies intoxication with the spirit, separation from the material world, drunkenness of love, companionship of comrades, and ecstasy in the presence of the Beloved.[21] In some poems, such as in "Sacred Wine," this metaphor is explicit:

How can I give up such a red, red drink?
Not from earth, from a wine press in nowhere.
The verses written on my cup in ink
promise this wine heals death, shame, and despair.
It comes from Tabriz, gushes out from there.
It's what I yearn for, my heaven down here.

People of Damnation brings together poems on another theme that has most often been overlooked by scholars: universal salvation. Rumi addresses those who are condemned in Islam and assures them of salvation. The damned are all saved in Rumi's poetic imagination. In the poem "Stones Come Alive" Rumi refers to traditional sayings (hadith) of the Prophet Muhammad in which he is reported by some scholars to have condemned the land of Najd as the dwelling-place of Satan.[22] According to this tradition, the people of Najd are cursed. They are the people of damnation. Nonetheless, Rumi invites the people of Najd into paradise on the Day of Judgment:

• xv

Peace! Praise! on the people of damnation.
. . . .
A king with glowing cheeks has now appeared!
The rocks, the stones wake up and they come near
to bless the day when everyone will hear
his Word. From that Word his command is clear.

Rumi insists that the Day of Judgment will bring redemption to all, universal salvation. In "Saved on Judgment Day" the hypocrites who are taunted in the Qur'an as those who will be found wanting are saved when Shams-e Tabrizi lets them borrow some of his light.

The ones who shall be saved know what to do:
Reach out for generosity from you.
Whoever stumbles on calamity
will have your gifts, and your protection too.

The Qur'an (sura 7) relates the story of the wicked people of Madyan, who reject God's prophet Shuaib's commandment to worship only one

God and to be honest in their business dealings. The people of Madyan are then destroyed by earthquakes and thunderbolts from heaven. Rumi assures us, however, that they too will be saved on the Day of Judgment in "You, People of Madyan!":

> Without judgment, our worth is certified.
> Gardens above gardens, above gardens.
> You who were lost: Come! Make your home inside.
> He raises every soul to ecstasy.

The Day of Judgment according to Rumi is a day of laughter, not fear. In "Divine Springtime" he writes:

> Spring is here, full of promises. The threat
> of winter melts, and God forgives our sins.
> He said it: "I have canceled every debt."
> Smile! Take your portion. This is the best step.

The part titled The Victory brings together poems in which Rumi writes of the joys and triumphs of salvation. Remembering that it is a universal salvation, all of humanity can partake of this victory. In "The Victory" Rumi celebrates:

> The victory of God is here!
> The Day that we all craved.
> Gather, friends! Walk in with the saved.
> He is calling. Forget your cares.

From Poetry to Poetry

The poems of Rumi present unique challenges to any translator. We are told by legend that Rumi composed his poems in the midst of meditation and spiritual practice spontaneously, in a state of high ecstasy. They were written down in the moment by his students. He did not revise or edit his poetic creations or correct their meter or rhyme. They were preserved untouched.

If these traditions are to be believed, then the poems of Rumi are the products of raw inspiration as he struggled to express his love. In "Divine Springtime," Rumi says as much. He breaks off in the middle of the poem to ask God (or perhaps Shams, one is never sure which) to give him words:

My Desire! Give me strength. Let these rhymes come.
My thoughts are pure, but my words come undone.
Speech is my teacher, but love strikes me dumb.

In this sense, the English translator is presented in the original Arabic with first drafts of poems, not polished and edited masterpieces intended for publication. However, the strength of the poems is found in their spontaneity, their natural language, and their ecstatic mood—not in literary perfection. Like many Sufi poems, Rumi's Arabic poems are often difficult to understand in the original language and are open to any number of interpretations.

While the translators must struggle with all of these technical issues, the goal is to make the poems comprehensible in a new language and beautiful, capturing the spirit of the original. We become Rumi's editors as the poems are prepared for publication for the first time in English. Interpretation is inevitable, and so we had to become inspired or risk losing the meaning of the poems. In the case of this volume, two translators had to share inspiration—returning repeatedly to the Arabic to explore alternate readings and meanings—to construct a meaningful English rendition of the poems.

In this volume, as in *Love Is My Savior*, the translation is the product of collaboration between an Arabic scholar and writer, Nesreen Akhtarkhavari, and an English-speaking poet, Anthony A. Lee, who knows no Arabic at all. Our method of translation began with Akhtarkhavari translating each poem into English literally, preserving the original line structure. Lee edited the lines to ensure the construction of acceptable poems in English. The first drafts were then returned to Akhtarkhavari for comment and correction; and then, back and forth, until both were satisfied that the translated poems were accurate and well-constructed. Throughout the process, the meaning of the Arabic was carefully explained to Lee and frequently edited by Akhtarkhavari to ensure that the images and words used in English were as clear and as powerful as those in the source text. Then, the poems were grouped, and titles that reflected the content were added to help Western readers more easily approach the poems.

The goal of this translation was to construct poem in English that were successful on their own terms, while remaining as close and true to the form and meaning of the originals as possible. In most cases, the poems are translated line for line, so the Arabic reader can follow in the original language on the facing page. Rhyme and meter are such vital and integral aspects of Rumi's poetry—of all classical poetry—that the translators felt that both had to be acknowledged. However, Arabic scanning has been, in most cases, exchanged for iambic pentameter, a familiar English convention. While foreign to Arabic poetry, this scheme gives the poems a rhythm that is comfortable to the English reader. English has fewer opportunities for rhyme as compared with Arabic due to the root system of Arabic syntax and its vast vocabulary. Yet, every effort was made to include rhyme prominently in the English versions.

Translating poems from one language to another might seem futile. Every poem is a condensed form of language that captures the essence of human experience, which must appeal to the mind as much as to the heart with images and words with deep cultural value on multiple levels, suggesting multiple meanings. Even if we were to alter a poem in its original language and change a few words here and there, we would destroy the beauty of the work. How then can all the words of a poem be changed to a different language, with their foreign connotations and associations, and preserve anything of the original meaning and effect?

However, poetry is not just words. It is the construct of language that we turn to when words fail to express our thoughts and feelings adequately. It is an attempt to move beyond words to communicate states of mind and spirit that cannot be captured by language but which nonetheless must be expressed. The poem must conjure emotion in the reader. Perhaps it is possible to find those emotions—across languages, across cultures, across time—and to translate poems and find the words in the target language to move new readers. This is possible not by translating words but by looking behind to the concepts, the music, and the images to find the essence of the poem. Of course, the quality of the result depends upon the knowledge of the Arabic scholar and the skill of the English poet. This method of translation is relatively uncommon in academia but has recently becoming appreciated.

These poems must be approached and read as poems, verses of insight, even in translation. Each poem invites us to enter a world that is unique and beyond time and space, the mystic universe of Rumi, allowing us to be transfixed by the beauty of his spiritual experiences, understood on no other terms but their own. We hope that these translations will accomplish that goal for their readers as intensely, and indeed as ecstatically, as the original Arabic poems do for their readers.

NOTES

1. For details about Rumi's mystic life, see Ibrahim Gamard and A. G. Rawan Farhadi, *The Quatrains of Rumi: Ruba'iyat-Jalaluddin Muhammad Balkhi-Rumi* (Sufi Dari Books, 2008).

2. An alternate spelling of al-Tabrizi's name is Shams-e Din Tabrizi, which literally translates as the Sun of Religion from Tabriz.

3. Shams was a poor, wandering dervish, about sixty years old, and Rumi was a thirty-seven-year-old wealthy, distinguished scholar with a school and many disciples.

4. See Annemarie Schimmel, *The Triumphal Sun: A Study of the Works of Jalaloddin Rumi* (New York: State University of New York Press, 1993).

5. For details about Rumi's life see Franklin D. Lewis, *Rumi: Past and Present, East and West; The Life, Teachings, and Poetry of Jalâl al-Din Rumi*, 2nd ed. (London: Oneworld, 2007). Unless otherwise noted, the account of Rumi's life relies on Lewis's book. See especially, 9–37.

6. A ghazal is a lyric poem with fixed number of verses and repeated rhyme, typically on the theme of love. The title *Divan-e Shams-e Tabrizi* translates to the collection of poems for, of, or by Shams-e Tabrizi.

7. For further details about Arabic verses and prose sections in Rumi's works, see Ibrahim Gamard, "About Rumi's Arabic Poetry," http://www.dar-al-masnavi.org/about-arabic-poetry.html.

8. A qasida is a classical monometered poem with every verse ending with the same rhyme. This recognition of the quatrains construction of the lines

were first brought to Akhtarkhavari's attention by Aref Awad al-Helal, a Jordanian poet and linguist who reviewed with her the Arabic poems in the manuscript.

9. These scholars include al-Harith al-Muhasibi (781–857), Abu al-Fayd Sauban ibn Ibrahim al-Misri, better known as Dhul-Nun al-Misri (796–861), Abu-Yazid Surushan al-Bistami, known as Bayazid Bistami (804–875), Abu al-Qasim ibn Muhammad al-Junayd al-Baghdadi, known as Sayyid al-Taifa (835–910), Abu al-Muġiṭ al-Ḥusayn ibn Manṣur al-Ḥallag [Hallaj] (858–922), and Abu al-Hamid Muhammad al-Ghazali (1058–1111).

10. These authors include Abu Nasr 'Abdallah ibn 'Ali al-Sarraj (d. 988), Mohammad ibn 'Ali Abu Talib al-Makki (d. 996), Abu 'Abd al-Rahman al-Solami (d. 1021), Ahmad ibn 'Abd Allah ibn Ahmad ibn Ishāq a-Mihrani al-Asfahani known as Abu Nu`aym al-Isfahani (d. 1038), and 'Abd al-Karim ibn Huzan Abu al-Qasim al-Qushayri (d. 1072).

11. Omar Khayyam is Ghiyath al-Din Abu al-Fath 'Umar ibn Ibrahim al-Khayyam Nishapuri (1048–1131), a Persian mathematician, astronomer, philosopher, Sufi, and poet best known in the West for his Rubaiyat (*robaiyat*, quatrains). Hakim Abu'l-Majd Majedud ibn Adam Sana'i Ghaznavi, also known as Sana'i, died between 1131 and 1141. Abu-Ḥamid ibn Abu-Bakar Ibrahim (1145–1220), better known by his pennames Farid ud-Din and 'Attar, was a Persian poet, theoretician of Sufism, and hagiographer from Nishapaur.

12. For an explanation of the images used in Rumi's poetry, see Schimmel, *The Triumphal Sun*.

13. Abu 'Abd-Allah Muḥammad ibn 'Ali ibn Muhammad ibn 'Arabi al-Ḥatimi at-Ta'i (1165–1240), or Ibn Arabi, was an Arab Andalusian scholar, Sufi mystic, poet, and philosopher.

14. For a detailed discussion of the possible encounter between Ibn Arabi and Rumi, see Omid Safi, "Did the Two Oceans Meet? Connections and Disconnections between Ibn al-Arabi and Rumi," *Journal of the Muhyiddin Ibn Arabi Society* 26 (1999): 55–88.

15. Adnan Karaismailoglu, "Mulana Jallaladin Muhammad Rumi," in *Rumi and His Sufi Path of Love*, ed. M. Fatih Citlak and Huseyin Bingul (Istanbul: Light, 2007), 47.

16. Abu al-Tayyib Ahmad ibn al-Husayn al-Mutanabbi al-Kindi (915–965)

was one of the greatest poets in the Arabic language. For examples of al-Mutanabi's poems in Rumi's work, see "About Rumi's Arabic Poetry."

17. *Kulliyat Shams ya Divan Kabir*, edited by Badi u-Zaman Furuzanfar (Tehran: Amir Kabir Press, 1957).

18. Daylam is a region near Gîlân in Persia where the people are known for their beautiful curly hair.

19. Lewis, *Rumi: Past and Present, East and West*, 320–23.

20. See Ibrahim Gamard's explanation of homoerotic and wine metaphors in "Apparently Irreligious Verses in the Works of Mawlana Rumi," http://dar-al-masnavi.org/apparently-irreligious-verses.html.

21. See Lewis, *Rumi: Past and Present, East and West*, 324–26.

22. Among the best known of these is one hadith related by Imam al-Bukhari in which Ibn Umar is reported to have said: "The Prophet (Peace be upon him) mentioned, 'O God, give us your blessings in our Syria. O God, give us your blessings in our Yemen.' The people said, 'And in our Najd?' and he said, 'O God, give us your blessings on our Syria. O God, give us your blessings in our Yemen.' They said, 'And on our Najd?' and I believe that he said on the third time, 'There will be earthquakes and afflictions there, and the horns of Satan [*qarn al-shaytan*] will come out there.'"

You Are Beautiful!

أنتَ جَمِيلٌ

بَشِّرْهُمْ بِنَظْرَةٍ

إِنَّ طَيِّبَ الرِّضَا، بَشَّرَ أَهْلَ الهَوَى
كُلَّ زَمَانٍ لَكُمْ، خِلعَةُ رُوحٍ جَدِيدْ
بَشِّرْهُمْ نَظْرَةً، يُتبِعُهُمْ نَظْرَةً
مِن رَشَأٍ سَيِّدٍ، لَيْسَ لَهُ مِن نَدِيدْ

The Glance

Our Healer brought good news to those who love:

Each moment, you can put on a new soul!

He promised us his glance, and then he glanced.

My Master! Brightest Star! The only goal.

يا مَليحاً

يا مَليحاً زَادَهُ الرَّحمنُ إحسَاناً جَديدْ

يا مُنيراً زَادَهُ نُوراً عَلى نُورٍ مَزيدْ

كُلُّ ذِي رُوحٍ يُفَدّي فِي هَواكَ رُوحَهُ

كُلُّ بُستانٍ أنيقٍ فِي جَنَاكَ مُسْتَفيدْ

لَسْتُ أُنْكِرْ مَا ذَكَرْتُمْ، البَقَاءُ فِي الفَنَا

كُلُّ مَنْ أبْدى جَميلاً لَيْسَ يبْعُدْ أنْ يُعيدْ

You Are Beautiful!

Beautiful! And God increased your beauty.

Radiant! He poured his light on your light.

Every soul must do its duty—offer

self as a sacrifice for your love. Then,

your grace will give life to every garden.

I heard your word: "In dying, I will live!"

You gave me grace, and you have more to give.

نَجْمَةُ الشَرْق

يَا مَنْ نَعْمَاهُ غَيرُ مَعْدُودْ

وَالسَّعْيُ لَدَيْهِ غَيرُ مَرْدُودْ

قَدْ أَكْرَمَنَا وَقَدْ دَعَانَا

كَي نَعْبُدَهُ وَنِعْمَ مَعْبُودْ

لا يَطْلُبُ حَمْدَنَا لِفَخْرٍ

بَل يَجْعَلُنَا بِذَاكَ مَحْمُودْ

قَدْ بَشَّرَ بِاللِقَاءِ صِدْقَاً

مِنْ حَضْرَتِهِ الكَريمُ مَوْرُودْ

وَالوَعْدُ مِنَ الحَبِيبِ حُلْوٌ

وَالسَّعْيُ إِلى السُّعُودِ مَسْعُودْ

«خاصا سعدي كه أو بهر دم

صد دل بسعود خويش بربود»*

6 .

---

*البيت الأخير باللغة الفارسية وترجمته، «خاصة سعدي الذي كلما تنفس علّق ألف قلب بسعود ذاته»، و»سعود» يرجع هنا إلى "سعد السعود" ألمع نجم في كوكبة الدلو ويسترشد به للدلالة على موقع النجوم الأخرى. أما «سعدي (1210-1229) أبو محمد مصلح الدين بن عبد الله الشيرازي، فهو الشاعر الفارسيّ الصوفيّ المعروف.

Eastern Star

It's you! Whose gifts are beyond my counting,

who never turns his back on any prayer,

who is gracious, who calls me to worship

your name, which I adore beyond compare.

He doesn't seek my praise, nor boast of it.

In praise, it's my own honor I repair.

He brings good news: the gift of reunion.

Look by his side! I find God's bounty there.

Beloved! Promises from you are sweet.

In joy, I reach for Su'ud,* your star.

Just like that Sa'di,† who could always hook

a hundred hearts to his own brilliant star.‡

————————————

*Sa'd al-Su'ūd (literally, "luckiest of the lucky") is the traditional Arabic name of the brightest star in a double-star cluster in the constellation Aquarius in Beta Aquarii. It is the anchor point from which other stars are charted.

†Abu-Muhammad Muslih al-Din bin Abdullah Shirazi (1210–1292), known as Sa'di, was a famed Persian Sufi poet.

‡The last two lines are Persian lines that were included in the selection.

أُقْتُلْنِي الآنَ

هَذَا سَيّدِيْ هَذَا سَنَدِيْ

هَذَا سَكَنِيْ هَذَا مَدَدِيْ

كَنَفِيْ هَذَا عَمَدِيْ

هَذَا أَزَلِيْ هَذَا أَبَدِيْ

يَا مَنْ وَجْهُهُ ضِعْفُ القَمَرِ

يَا مَنْ قَدُّهُ ضِعْفُ الشَّجَرِ

يَا مَنْ زَارَنِيْ وَقْتَ السَّحَرِ

يَا مَنْ عِشْقُهُ نُوْرُ النَّظَرِ

يَا مُنْبَسِطاً فِيْ تَرِبِيَتِيْ

يَا مُبْتَشِراً فِيْ تَهْنِئَتِيْ

إِنْ كُنْتَ تَرى أَنْ تَقْتُلَنِيْ

يَا قَاتِلَنَا أَنْتَ دِيَّتِيْ

Kill Me Now

Master! You're my Teacher, and you're my Strength,

my Guide, my Savior in calamity.

More, you are my shelter, my protection,

my eternal life—all that I can be.

For me, your holy face is twice the moon!

You are taller than every cypress tree!

You came to me at night before the dawn,

your love the only light my eyes could see.

So generous! You taught me all I know.

You were so happy singing praise of me.

So, go ahead and kill me, if you like.

My murderer, you're Immortality.

لا أَقْوَى عَلَى الِانْتِظَارِ

فَإِنْ وَفَّقَ اللّهُ الكَرِيمَ وِصَالَكُمْ

وَعَايَنَ رُوحِيْ حُسْنَكُمْ وَجَمَالَكُمْ

تَصَدَّقْتُ بِالرُّوحِ العَزِيزِ لِشُكْرِهَا

فَبِاللّهِ ارحَموا ذُلِّيْ وَعِشْقِيْ، فَمَا لَكُمْ

إلى كَمْ أَقَاسِيْ هَجرَكُمْ وَفِرَاقَكُمْ؟

إلى كَمْ أُوانِسْ طَيفَكُمْ وَخَيالَكُمْ؟

تَنَاقَصَ صَبرِيْ بِازدِيَادِ مَلالَكُمْ

فَيَالَيتَني، أفنِيْ كَصَبرِيْ مَلالَكُمْ

عَمَى العَينَ مَنْ تِذْكَارِهَا حَرَكَاتُكُمْ

وَغَنْجَائِها وَيلاكُمْ وَدَلالُكُمْ

رَآنِي الهَوَى يَوماً أُلاعِبُ غَفْلَتِي

فَصَاحَ عَلَينَا صَيْحَةَ العِشْقِ وَا لَكُمْ

لَقَدْ جَاءَ مِنْ تَبرِيزَ رُوحٌ مُجَسَّمٌ

ألا فَانْثُرُوا فِيْ حُبِّ نَعْلَيْهِ مَالَكُمْ

I Can't Wait

God joined us in his generosity.

I saw your beauty and your majesty.

I sacrificed my soul so gratefully.

Have mercy on my love, my misery.

How much I suffered when you fled from me.

I am alone, with just your memory.

Your rejection doesn't end. I can't wait.

My patience drained! So, drain my life from me.

I go blind remembering our reverie—

me flirting in your teasing company.

Love found me idle in my ignorance.

He shouted (and his love surrounded me):

"A brilliant spirit has come from Tabriz.

Throw all you own at his feet—joyfully!"

السَّرَابُ

يَا شَبَهَ الطَّيْفِ لِيْ، أَنْتَ قَرِيبٌ بَعِيْدْ

جُملَةُ أَرْوَاحِنَا، تَغْمِسُ فِيمَا تُرِيْدْ

«نوبت آدم گذشت، نوبت مرغان رسيد

طبل قيامت زدند، خيز كه فرمان رسيد»*

أَنْتَ لَطِيفُ الفِعَالْ، أَنْتَ لَذِيْذُ المَقَالْ

أَنْتَ جَمَالُ الكَمَالْ، زِدْتَ فَهَلْ مِنْ مَزِيْدْ

جَاءَ أَوَانُ السُّرُورْ، زَالَ زَمَانُ الفُتُورْ

لَيْسَ لَدَينا غُرُورْ، يَا سَنَدِيْ لا تَحِيْدْ

هَلْ طَرَبٌ يَا غُلامْ؟، فَامْلَأِ الكَاسَ المُدَامْ

أَنْتَ بِدَارِ السَّلامْ، سَاكِنُ قَصْرٍ مَشِيْدْ

يَا لَمَعُ المَشْرِقِ، مِثْلُكَ لَمْ يُخْلَقِ

خُذْ بِيَدِيْ، أَرْتَقِيْ، نَحوَكَ، أَنْتَ المَجِيْدْ

اعْلَمْ أنَّ الغُبَارْ، مُرْتَفِعٌ بِالرِّيَاحْ

مِثْلُ هَوَاءٍ اخْتَفَى، وَسْطَ صَبَاحٍ جَدِيْدْ

---

*هذا البيت باللغة الفارسية معناه «لقد انتهى زمن البشر، وحل محلة زمن الطير، وقرعوا طبول القيامة، حين وصل الخطاب.»

Mirage

I see your shadow here, a far pathway.

So, take my soul, and then do as you may.

The time of man has passed. The birds have come.

I hear the bells of the Resurrection.*

Your rule is gentle and your words are sweet.

You are Beauty! Perfection! The straight way!

Now, joy has come. My hopeless days are done.

I have no pride: my Strength. I beg you, stay!

Wine boy! Come fill my cup. I am undone.

He's in the Palace of Peace—high away.

Bright light of the East! You're the only One.

Hold my hand. Lift me, as your glory may!

But like the dust raised, blown off by the wind,

my Love has disappeared, in light of day.

---

*The third and fourth lines are translated from Persian lines in the original poem.

زَلْزَلْتَ عَقْلِي

يَا مُنِيرَ البَدْرِ قَدْ أوْ ضَحْتَ فِيْ البِلْبَالِ بَالْ

بِالهَوَى زَلْزَلْتِنيْ وَالْعَقْلُ فِي الزِّلْزَالِ زَالْ

كَمْ أُنَادِي أنْظُرُونَا نَقْتَبِسْ مِنْ نُورِكُمْ؟

قَدْ رَجَعْنَا جَائِباً مِنْ نُورِ أنْوَارِ الجَلَالْ

مَنْ رَأى نُوراً أنِيساً يَمْلأُ الدُّنيا هَوَىَ

لِلسُّرَى مِنهُ جَمَالٌ لِلعِدى مِنْهُ مَلَالْ

كُلُّ أمْرٍ مِنْهُ حَقٌّ مُسْتَحَقٌّ، نَافِذٌ

يَنْفَعُ الأمْراضَ طُرّاً يَنْجَلِيْ مِنْهُ الكَلَالْ

مَنْ شَكَا مِغْلاقَ بَابٍ فَلِيَنَلْ مِفْتَاحَهْ

مَنْ شَكَا ضُرَّ الظَّمَأُ، فَلْيَسْتَقِي المَاءَ الزُّلَالْ

لَيْسَ ذَا أسْمَاءَ صِفْرٍ بَاطِلٍ سَمَّيْتُهُ

دَعْوَةُ التَّحْقِيقِ حَالٌ خُدْعَةُ الدُّنيا مُحَالْ

حَبَذا أسْواقُ أشْواقٍ رَبَتْ أرْبَاحُهَا

حَبَذا نُورٌ يَكُونُ الشَّمْسُ فِيه كَالهِلالْ

مَا عَلَيْكُمْ لَوْ سَهِرْتُمْ لَيْلَةً إلْفَ الهَوَى

رُبَّما تَلقَوْنَ ضَيْفاً يَعرِفُ لَيلَ الرِّحَالْ

يَا مُحِبّاً قُمْ تَنَادَمْ فَالمُحِبُّ لا يَنَامْ

يَا نَعُوساً قُمْ تَفَرَّجْ حُسْنَ رَبَّاتِ الحِجَالْ

I Lost My Mind

You light up the full moon! And you light me.

Trembling with love, I lose my mind again.

I shout, "Look here at me! I'll take your light."

I moved from one light to a greater light.

He fills the world with love. Who's seen such light?

To friends he's beauty—to enemies fright.

His command is certain; his word is right.

He heals my wounds, restores my soul's full might.

You say the door is closed? So, here's the key.

You say you die of thirst? He's clear water.

You named him. But he has no name. He's free.

His invitation—your transformation.

The world's mirage—a conjuration.

Would we could sell our love. We would be rich!

Would the sun were now a crescent in the sky.

Stay the night with love as your companion.

You might meet someone here just passing by.

Lover, wake! Get drunk with me. Love can't sleep.

Hey! Wake up! Watch the angels wander by.

كِدْتُ أفْقِدُ دِينِي

صُدْعُ الوَفَاءِ حَقّاً، مِنْ فَقدِكُمْ مُشَّوَش
وَجْهُ الوَلاءِ حَقّاً، مِنْ عَبرَتِي مُنَّقَش
القَلْبُ لَيْسَ يَلْقَى، نَادِيكَ، كَيْفَ يَصْبِرْ؟
الأُذْنُ لَيْسَ يَلْقَنْ، حَادِيكَ، كَيْفَ يَنْعَش؟

I Almost Lost My Faith

But when you walked away from me that day,

    I almost lost my faith.

My face is scarred by tears of loyalty.

The heart that cannot feel your welcome call

    finds no tranquility.

The ear that will not hear your midnight song

    has no vitality.

أنْقِذْنِي

عَمْرُكَ، يَا وَاحِداً، في دَرَجاتِ الكَمَالْ

قَدْ نَزَلَ الهَمُّ بِي، يَا سَنَدِيْ، قُمْ تَعَالْ

يَا فَرَحِي، يَا مُؤنِسِي، يَا قَمَرَ المَجْلِسِ

وَجهُكَ بَدْرٌ تَمامْ، رِيقُكَ خَمْرٌ حَلالْ

رُوحُكَ بَحْرُ الوَفَا، لَونُكَ لَمْعُ الصَّفَا

عَمْرُكَ لَوْلا التُّقَى، قُلْتَ أيَا ذَا الجَلالْ

تَسْكُنُ قَلْبَ الوَرَى، تُسْكِرُهُمْ بِالهَوَى

تُدْرِكُ مَا لا يُرَى، أنْتَ لَطِيفُ الخَيَالْ

تُسْكِنُ أرْواحَهُمْ، تُسْكِرُ أشْباحَهُمْ

تُجْلِسُهُمْ مَجْلِساً، فِيْهِ كُؤوسٌ ثِقَالْ

Rescue Me!

I swear by my life! You are perfection!
I'm grieving, my Sustainer. Rescue me!
My friend! My joy! Orb of our protection,
your mouth's nectar is sacred wine for me.
Your face is the moon's reflection.
Your color—pure light. Your soul—fidelity.

I swear by my life! But for fear of God,
I would call you the highest deity.
Dwell in my heart, and keep me drunk on love.
Your gentle gaze knows every mystery.
You're in me; you're my soul's intoxication.
Fill my cup with wine in your company.

The Agony of Love

عَذَابُ الحُبِّ

سِرُّ العِشْقِ

يَقُولُ العِشْقُ لِي سِرّاً: «تَنافَسْ واغْتَنِمْ بِرّاً
وَلا تَفْجُرْ وَلا تَهْجُرْ، وإلا تَبْتَئِسْ، تَنْدَمْ»
مَضَى فِي صَحْوَتِيْ يَوِمِيْ، وَفَاضَ السُّكْرُ فِي قَوْمِي
فَأَسْرِعْ وَاسقِنِيْ خَمْراً، حُمَيْرا تُشْبِهُ العَنْدَمْ

Love's Secret

Love told me a secret: struggle is the key.

    That's how you'll find love and gain dignity.

Don't rage at your lover. Don't turn and flee—

    you'll find yourself in utter misery.

All day I was sober, my friends all drunk.

So, hurry! Bring that blood-red wine to me.

عَذَابُ الحُبِّ

أُمسِيْ وَأُصْبِحُ بِالجَوَى أَتَعَذَّبُ

قَلْبِي عَلَى نَارِ الهَوَى يَتَقَلَّبُ

إِنْ كُنْتَ تَهْجُرُنِيْ تُهَذِّبُنِيْ بِهِ

أَنْتَ النُّهَى وَبَلاَكَ لا أَتَهَذَّبُ

مَا بَالُ قَلْبِكَ قَدْ قَسَى فَإِلَى مَتَى

أَبْكِيْ وَمِمَّا قَدْ جَرَى أَتَعَتَّبُ

مِمَّا أُحِبُّ بِأَنْ أَقُولَ فَدَيتِكُمْ

أَحْيَا بِكُمْ وَقَتِيلُكُمْ يَتَقَلَّبُ

وَأَشَرْتُمْ بِالصَّبْرِ لِي مُتَسَلِّياً

مَا هَكَذَا عِشْقِي بِهِ لا تَحْسِبوا

مَا عِشْتُ فِي هَذَا الفُرَاقِ سُوَيعَةً

لَوْلا لِقَاؤُكَ كُلَّ يَوْمٍ أَرْقُبُ

إِنِّي أَتُوبُ مُنَاجِياً وَمُنَادِياً

فَأَنَا المُسِيءُ بِسَيِّدِيْ وَالمُذْنِبُ

تَبْرِيزُ جَلَّ بِشَمْسِ دِينٍ سَيِّدِيْ

أَبْكِيْ دَماً مِمَّا جَنَيْتُ وَأَشْرَبُ

The Agony of Love

He begins my every day—and ends it.

My heart roasts in love's fire on a spit.

Forget me then! And I will learn the way.

No, without you I'll always go astray.

How long will your hard heart keep me grieving?

I cry and blame myself for your leaving.

I beg my life be sacrificed for you!

You are my life; without you I am dead.

You say I should use patience as my balm?

No, don't think that my love can be that calm.

I couldn't stand your loss for one moment

if I didn't think you'd return each dawn.

I repent! I shout. I beg, and I bray!

I'm guilty, I disgraced you every day.

Still, Tabriz shines with the Sun of Faith,* my Master.

I cry blood, and drink to forget my disaster.

_____

*In Arabic, "Sun of Faith" translates to Shams-e Din.

أَنْتُمُ الشَّمْسُ وَالقَمَرُ

أَنْتُمُ الشَّمْسُ وَالقَمَرْ، مِنْكُمُ السَّمْعُ وَالبَصَرْ
نَظَرَ القَلْبِ فِيكُمْ، بِكُمْ يَنْجَلِي النَّظَرْ
قُلْتُمُ الصَّبْرُ أَجْمَلْ، صَبَرَ العَبْدُ مَا انصَبَرْ
نَحْنُ أَبْنَاءُ وَقْتِنَا، رَحَمَ اللهُ مَنْ غَبَرْ
قَدِمُوا سَادَةُ الهَوَى، قُلْتُ يَا قَوْمِ، مَا الخَبَرْ؟
خَوَّفُونِي بِفِتْنَةٍ، وَأَشَارُوا إلى الحَذَرْ
قُلْتُ: «القَتْلُ فِي الهَوَى، بَرَكَاتٌ بِلا ضَرَرْ
جَرَّدَ العِشْقُ سَيْفَهُ، بَادِرُوا أُمَّةَ الفِكَرْ*
إِنَّ مَنْ عَاشَ بَعْدَ ذَا، ضَيَّعَ الوَقْتَ وَاحْتَكَرْ
نَفَخُوا فِي شِبَابَةٍ، حَمَلَ الرِّيحُ بِالشَّرَرْ
مَزَجَ النَّارَ بِالهَوَى، لَيْسَ يُبْقِي وَلا يَذَرْ
شَبِّبُوا لِي بِنَفْخَةٍ، يُسْكِرُ نَفْخَةَ السَّحَرْ»

---

*يعاتب «أمة الفكر» وهم فرق من المتصوفة رأوا في العقل والفكر طريقا إلى الله بدل العشق الإلهي.

You Are the Sun!

You are the sun! You are the moon! My ears!

My eyes! I look through you, and now I see.

You love patience. But you know patient as

a slave I cannot be! This is our time.

On those who've gone before, God have mercy.

Masters of Love came here. I said, "Teach me."

They spoke of fear and immorality.

"Take care," they said. "Be wise. That's our decree."

"I'm in love!" I said. "Death my life will be."

Love draws his sword and first slays sanity.*

The one who stays alive lives uselessly.

They played flutes. The wind grew hot and sparkled.

No water. He mixed fire with love unsteadily.

"Play on!" I said. "Keep me drunk for eternity."

.

---

*This is a rebuke to those Sufis who would prefer knowledge instead of love as the path to Divine.

يُهْرِقُ العِشْقُ دِمَاءَ

حَكَّمَ البَيْنُ بِمَوْتِيْ وَعَمَدْ

رَضِيَ الصَّدُّ بِحَيْنِيْ وَقَصَدْ

فَتَحَ الدَّهْرُ عُيُونَ حَسَدٍ

فَرَآنا بِفَنَاكُمْ وَحَسَدْ

يُهْرِقُ العِشْقُ دِمَاءً حُقِنَت

لَيْسَ لِلعِشْقِ قَرِيبٌ وَوَلَدْ

لَكِنِ المَوْتُ حَيَاةٌ لَكُمُ

لَكِنِ الفَقْرُ فَنَاءٌ وَرَغَدْ

سَافِرُوا في سَبِيلِ العِشْقِ مَعِي

لا تَخَافُنَّ ضَلالاً وَرَصَدْ

لا يَهُولَنَّكُمْ بُعْدُكُمْ

دُونَكُمْ وَفْدَ وِصَالٍ وَمَدَدْ

فَنَسِيمُ طَرَبٍ أوَّلَهُمْ

يَهَبُ المَالِكَ حَوْلاً وَجَلَدْ

There Will Be Blood

When you left me, you sentenced me to die.

You cast me out! You knew you sealed my fate.

There had appeared a jealous, evil eye

who saw me with you and was filled with hate.

Where there is love, nearby there will be blood.

Love will not spare father, and not son.

But death is everlasting life with you.

Poverty is the jewel your lovers won.

Come with me now. Come on the path of love.

Don't be afraid of sin or prying eyes.

Don't worry that you may be far from home.

Come! Find union. Salvation is the prize!

That magic breeze that stirred man's first passion

now gives his lovers strength and calms their lives.

بِلا نُورٍ

ظَنَنْتُمْ أَيَا عُذَّالُ أَنْ قَدْ عَدَلْتُمْ

تَظُنُّونَ أَنَّ الحَقَّ فِيمَا عَدَلْتُمْ

وَمَا ضَاءَ ذَاكَ البَدْرُ إِلَّا لِأَهْلِهِ

وَغَادَرَكُمْ أَنْوَارُهُ فَضَلِلْتُمْ

فَمَا مَلَّ مَنْ ذَاقَ الصَّبَابَةَ وَالهَوَى

وَإِنَّكُمُ مَا ذُقْتُمْ فَمَلِلْتُمْ

وَإِنْ ذُقْتُمُ مَا ذُقْتُمُوهُ بِحَقِّهَا

ولا مَشْرَبَ العُشَّاقِ يَوْماً وَصَلْتُمْ

You're Empty

Complainer! You call yourself just and fair.

You think you can denounce me everywhere.

But moonlight shines only on the faithful.

So, you can't see his might. You're unaware.

I've tasted love. So, I'm never thirsty.

You're empty, since you never found that place.

The cup from which you drink is such a waste.

You never found the spring his lovers taste.

تَزَيَّن

العِشْقُ يَقُولُ لِي: «تَزَيَّنْ
الزِّينَةُ عِنْدَنا» تَيَقَّنْ

لا تَنْظُرْ غَيْرَنا فَتَعْمَى

لا تَلْهَ عَنِ اليَقِينِ بِالظَّنْ

لا عَيْشَ لِخائِفٍ كَئِيبٍ

لا تَبْرَحْ عِنْدَنا فَتَأْمَنْ

مَنْ كُنْتُ هَوَاهُ كَيْفَ يَهْلِكْ؟

مَنْ كُنْتُ مُنَاهُ كَيْفَ يَحْزَنْ؟

العَقْلُ رَسُولُنا إِلَيْكُمْ

ذَاكَ حَسَنٌ وَنَحْنُ أَحْسَنْ

أَخْشَوْشِنْ بِالبَلا وَأَرْضَى

فَالهَجْرُ مِنَ البَلاءِ أَخْشَنْ

مَنْ رَامَ إِلى العُلا عُرُوجاً

هَذا سَبَبٌ إِلَيْهِ يَرْكَنْ

يَا مُضْطَرِباً تَعالَ وَافْلَحْ

فِي مَسْكِنِنَا ونِعْمَ مَسْكَنْ

Put on Your Jewels

My Lover says to me: "Put on your jewels."

But you know that I have your jewels in me!

Don't look at any other. You'll go blind.

Don't lose your faith studying uncertainty.

Don't live your life in fear and misery.

Don't leave the safety of my company.

I am love, and my love in you is life.

I am desire; desire is not sad.

Yes, your mind will find me eventually.

That's good. But look! You're standing next to me!

Learn to suffer calamity and smile.

My absence is the worst catastrophe.

If you want to climb the highest mountain,

you know that you will reach your goal through me.

If you're lost here, make your way to my house.

Come! What a wonderful home it will be.

طَرِيْقُ العِشْقِ

أطَيَبُ الأعْمَارَ عُمْرٌ في طَرِيقِ العاشِقِيْنْ

غَمْزُ عَيْنٍ مِنْ مِلاحٍ في وِصَالٍ مُسْتَبِيْنْ

رُؤيَةُ المَعْشُوقِ يَوماً في مَقامٍ مُوحِشٍ

زَادَ طِيباً مِنْ جِنانٍ في قِيَانٍ حُورِ عِيْنْ

عَفِّرُوا مِنْ تُرْبِ بَابٍ بُغْيَةً وَجْهِي مَدّاً

فَهْيَ زَادَتْ لُطْفَها عِنْدِي مِنَ المَاءِ المَعِيْنْ

غَارَ جِسْمِي أنْ يَرَاهُ عَاذِلٌ أو عَاذِرٌ

إنَّهُ يَحْكِي صِفَاتاً مِنْ صِفَاتِ شَمْسِ دِيْنْ

حَبَّذَا سُكْرٌ حَيَاتِيٌّ مُزِيلٌ لِلْحَيَا

اشرَبُوا أصْحَابَنا تَسْتَمْسِكُوا الحَقَّ المُبِيْنْ

سَيّداً مَولاً كَرِيماً عَالِماً مُسْتَيْقِظَاً

اسْتَرَقَّ العَبْدَ ذَاكَ الطَّاهِرُ الرُّوحُ الأمِيْنْ

حَبَّذا ظِلّاً ظَلِيلاً مِنْ نَخِيلٍ بَاسِقٍ

آمِنٍ مِنْ كُلِّ خَوفٍ أو بَلاءٍ أو مَكِيْنْ

تَمْرُهُ يُصْفِي عُقُولاً كُدِّرَتْ أنوارُها

فَاعْجِبُوا مِنْ مُسْكِرٍ مُسْتَكْثِرِ الرَّأي الرَّزِيْنْ

The Path of Love

The best of life is on the path of love:

a black-eyed maiden's wink, consent to meet.

I don't find her on some deserted street

but in gardens with others just as sweet.

They sweep out the dust—my invitation!

She is so kind, and I have more to drink.

My body hides from blaming eyes—Salvation!

—with traces of love for Shams's station!

O Shams-e Din!

I want to get drunk. End my hesitation.

Drink, my friends! You will know salvation.

My Master, he's truth, generosity!

My Trusted Lord! Give me divinity.

I became a slave to his purity.

I sought the shadow of his tall palm tree.

Now I'm safe from fear and calamity.

His dates I use to heal my half-lit mind.*

Drink gives me wisdom of a different kind.

---

*This is a reference to palm wine, which, like all wines, is forbidden in Islam.

الهَوَى وَالجَوَى

يَا عاشِقِينَ المَقْصَدُ، سِيحُوا إلى مَا تُرْشَدُوا
وَاسْتَقْتِشُوا مَنْ يُسْعِدُ، يَلْقَونَ أيْنَ السَّيّدُ
العِشْقُ نُورٌ مُرْتَفِعْ، والسِيرُ نِعْمَ المُكْتَرَعْ
نِهْرُ الهَوَى لا يَنْقَطِعْ، نَارُ الهَوَى لا تَخْمُدُ
لا عِشْقَ إلا بالجَوى، مَنْ كَانَ فِي سُقِمِ الهَوَى
إنْ قِيلَ طَارَ في الهَوا، لا تُنْكِروا لا تُبْعِدوا
العِشْقُ مَا فِي رِقِّهِ، خَيرٌ لَكُم مِن عِتْقِهِ
جَفْنٌ بَكَى في عِشْقِهِ، لا تَحْسِبُوهُ يَرْمَدُ
أمْرُ المُحِبِينَ اِنْطَوَى، أمراضُهُمْ خَيْرُ الدّوا
مَا لَمْ يَضِلُّوا في الهَوَى، لا تَزْعَمُوا أنْ يَهْتَدوا
أصْحَابِنا لا تَيْأسُوا، بَعْدَ الجَوى مُسْتَأنَسْ
غَيْرَ الهَوَى لا تَلْبَسُوا، غَيْرَ الهَوى لا تَرْتَدوا
سِحْرُ الهَوَى مَعْقُودَةٌ، نَارُ الجَوَى مَوقُودَةٌ
ذا نِعْمَةٌ مَفْقُودَةٌ، حِرمانَ مَنْ لا يَجْهَدُ
نَادَيْتُ يَومَ المُلْتَقَى، إذْ حَارَ عَقْلِي وَالْتُقَى
هَذَا بَقَاءٌ في البَقَا، هَذَا نَعِيمٌ سَرْمَدُ
إنْ فَاتَكُمْ لا تَفْعَلُوا، واسْتَفْتِشُوهُ وَاعْقِلُوا
لا تَرْقُدُوا، لا تَأكُلُوا ، مَا لَمْ تَروا لا تَعْبُدُوا

Love and Pain

Lovers of Mecca! Take the path of his will!

Seek joy! You'll find it with my Master still.

Love is a holy light. Come drink your fill.

This river flows eternal with love's spill.

Love is a fire that will never wane.

Love brings death and pain. If you fall ill

with love, then you can fly. You won't sit still!

You're free. But, better be a slave of love.

The eye that cries for love does not waste tears.

See! The lover's cure is the love he fears.

To find direction, first get lost in love.

Man, don't despair. After the pain of love,

you'll find his company—when love appears!

Then, wear no clothes. Wear nothing else but love.

A magic spell: the fire of love burning.

This bounty only reaches those who strived.

On the Day of his Judgment, I was gone

astray. He touched my heart. I was revived

that day. I found eternal life that way.

I had arrived in Paradise to stay.

You missed him; keep looking! Be wise, I say.

Find him. Don't eat. Don't sleep. Don't stop to pray.

ذَابَ قَلْبِي

يَا صَغِيرَ السِّنِّ يَا رَطْبَ البَدَنْ

يَا قَرِيبَ العَهْدِ مِنْ شُرْبِ اللَّبَنْ

هَاشِمِيَّ الوَجْهِ، تُرْكِيَّ القَفَا

دَيْلَمِيَّ* الشَّعْرِ، رُومِيَّ الذَّقَنْ

رُوحُهُ رُوحِي وَرُوحِي رُوحُهُ

مَنْ رَأَى رُوحَينِ عَاشَا فِي بَدَنْ؟

صَحَّ عِنْدَ النَّاسِ أَنِّي عَاشِقٌ

غَيْرَ أَنْ لَمْ يَعْرِفُوا عِشْقِي بِمَنْ

اقْطَعُوا شَمْلِيْ وَإِنْ شِئْتُمْ صِلُوا

كُلُّ شَيْءٍ مِنْكُمْ عِنْدِيْ حَسَنْ

ذَابَ مِمَّا فِي مَتَاعِي وَطَنِيْ

وَمَتَاعِيْ بَادَ مِمَّا فِي وَطَنْ

---

*إحدى الشعوب الإيرانية التي عاشت في شمال الهضبة الإيرانية. بلاد الديلم أو بلاد جيلان واقعة في الجنوب الغربي من شاطئ بحر الخزر. عرف أهلها بجمال شعرهم وتموجه.

My Heart Melts

You are so young, and your body so fresh.

Not far from days when you were drinking milk.

A princely face, and Turkish from behind,

Daylam hair,* a chin like Romans carry.

Your soul is my soul, and my soul is yours.

Who has seen two souls in one body?

Of course, they all know that I am in love.

But they don't know who my love might be.

Run away from me! Or stay, if you will.

Whatever you give will be fine with me.

I melted down my heart to find a home.

Now, my heart melts for who is in my home.

_____

*Daylam is a region in Persia near Gîlân where the people are known for their beautiful curly hair.

تَعَالَ إلى النُّورِ

أيُّهَا النُّورُ في الفُؤادِ تَعَالْ

غَايَةَ الجِدِّ والمُرَادِ! تَعَالْ

أنتَ تَدْري حَياتُنا بِيَدَيْكْ

لا تُضَيِّقْ عَلى العِبَادِ، تَعَالْ

أيُّها العِشْقُ، أيُّها المَعْشُوقُ

حُلْ عَنِ الصَّدِّ والعِنَادِ، تَعَالْ

يا سُلَيْمانُ ذي الهَداهِدْ لَكْ

فَتَفَقَّدْ بِالافْتِقَادِ، تَعَالْ

أيُّها السَّابِقُ الَّذِي سَبَقَتْ

مِنْكَ مَصْدُوقَةُ الوَدَادِ، تَعَالْ

فَمِنَ الهَجْرِ ضَجَّتْ الأَرْواحْ

أنجِزْ العَوْدَ يا مَعَادُ، تَعَالْ

اسْتُرِ العَيْبَ وابْذُلِ المَعْرُوفَ

هَكَذَا عَادَةُ الجَوَادِ، تَعَالْ

طُفْتُ فِيكَ البِلاَدَ يا قَمَراً

بِيْ مُحِيطاً وَبِالبِلادِ تَعَالْ

أنتَ كَالشَّمْسِ إذْ دَنَتْ وَنَأَتْ

يَا قَرِيباً عَلى البِعَادِ، تَعَالْ

Come to the Light

You are the light of my full heart. Come!

The goal of my search, my longing. Come!

You know my life is in your hand.

Do not torment your worshippers. Come!

You are my love, my Beloved.

No rejection. No more coldness. Come!

Solomon! All wisdom is from you.

Remember me, and come by here. Come!

You are high, the first among us.

You give me love and true friendship. Come!

My soul weeps in separation.

So, bring on the Day of Judgment. Come!

Conceal my sins and favor me.

That is your generosity. Come!

You are the Moon; you guided me.

You shine on me and on the land. Come!

You're the sun, so near then so far.

My Love, so close, so far away. Come!

Wine of Reunion

خَمْرُ التَّلاقِي

الخَمْرُ المُقَدَّسُ

كَيْفَ أَتُوبُ يَا أَخِي مِن سَكَرٍ كَأُرْجُوانْ؟
لَيْسَ مِنَ التُّرَابِ بَلْ مِعْصَرَةٌ بِلا مَكَانْ
خُطَّ عَلى كُؤُوسِها كِتَابَةٌ شَارِحَةٌ
يَا مَنْ يَشْرَبُها مِنَ المَمَاتِ وَالهَوَانْ
مِن تَبْرِيزَ نَبْعُهُ، مَنْبَتُهُ وَيَنْعُهُ
فَها إِلَيْها جَانِبٌ، وَجَانِبٌ مِنَ الجِنَانْ

Sacred Wine

Brother!

How can I give up such a red, red drink?

Not from earth, from a wine-press in nowhere.

The verses written on my cup in ink

promise this wine heals death, shame, and despair.

It comes from Tabriz, gushes out from there.

It's what I yearn for, my heaven down here.

خَمْرُ التَّلاقِي

نَشْرْنَا فِي رَبِيعِ الوَصْلِ بِالوَرْدِ

حَنَانِينَا فَنِعْمَ الزَّوْجُ وَالفَرْدِ

نَخَافُ العَيْنَ تَرْمِينَا بِسُوءٍ

فَيَا دَاوُدُ قَدِّرْ حَلْقَةَ السَّرْدِ*

أَلَا يَا سَاقِياً هَاتِ الحُمَيَّا

لِتَكْفِينَا عَنَاءَ الحَرِّ وَالبَرْدِ

وَأَسْكِرْنَا بِكَاسَاتٍ عِظَامٍ

فَإِنَّ السُّكْرَ دَفْعَ الهَمِّ وَالحَرْدِ

وَأَعْتِقْنَا بِخَمْرٍ مِنْ هُمُومٍ

وَجَازِيْ هَمَّنَا بِالدَّفْعِ وَالطَّرْدِ

46 •

---

* سورة سبا (34) آية 10-11: «أَنِ اعْمَلْ سَابِغَاتٍ وَقَدِّرْ فِي السَّرْدِ، وَاعْمَلُوا صَالِحًا. إِنِّي بِمَا تَعْمَلُونَ بَصِيرٌ.»

Wine of Reunion

Blessed each alone! Twice blessed in union!

We're sown here in this spring of tenderness!

Evil eyes want to end our communion.

David! Let the nail fit the hole in the shield.*

Wine boy! Bring the wine of reunion.

Protect us from heat and cold location.

Let us drink from your sacred cup! Ease our

troubled minds with wine's intoxication.

Free us, with wine, from our consternation.

Take away our fear and hesitation.

---

*See Qur'an 34:10-11: "And We certainly gave David from Us bounty. [We said], 'O mountains, repeat [Our] praises with him, and the birds [as well].' And We made pliable for him iron, [Commanding him], 'Make full coats of mail and calculate [precisely] the links, and work [all of you] righteousness. Indeed I, of what you do, am Seeing.'"

نِعْمَ القِيَامُ

أَقْبَلَ السّاقِي عَلَيْنا حامِلاً كَأْسَ المُدَامْ

فَاشْرَبُوا مِنْ كَأْسِ خُلْدٍ وَاتْرُكُوا كُلَّ الطّعَامْ

اشْبَعوا مِنْ غَيْرِ أَكْلٍ واسْمَعوا مِنْ غَيْرِ أُذْنِ

وَانْطِقُوا مِنْ غَيْرِ حَرْفٍ وَاسْكُنُوا تَمَّ الكَلَامْ

أَيُّها العُشّاقُ طِيبوا وَاسْكَرُوا مِنْ كَأْسِنَا

وَارْكَبُوا ظَهْرَ المَعالِي وَادْخُلُوا بَيْنَ الزّحَامْ

انْهَضُوا، نَادى المُنادِي: الصّلا أَيْنَ الرِّجالْ؟

جَاءَكُمْ نَادى القِيامَةُ في الهَوى، نِعْمَ القِيَامْ

اشْرَبُوا سُقْياً لَكُمْ، ثُمَّ اطرَبُوا غُنْماً لَكُم

إِنَّ هَذَا يَوْمُ عِيدٍ، عَيِّدوا بَعْدَ الصِّيَامْ

وَافِقُونا، وافِقُونا في طَرِيقِ الاِتِّحاذْ

إِنَّما نَحْنُ كَنَهْرٍ، فَرِّقُوهُ والسّلامْ

يَا نَدِيمِي، سَلْ سِبيلاً نَحْوَ عَيْنِ السّلْسَبِيلِ

قُمْ لَنا نَفْتَحْ جِناناً مِنْ جِنانٍ يَا غُلامْ

He Resurrected You

The wine boy holds your cup of wine. He's here!

Drink for eternity. No other food.

Feast without eating, and hear with no ear.

Speak without speaking. Be silent. No words.

Lover, drink from my cup. Be healed and cheer!

Ride on waves of glory. Join our company.

He calls us to prayer. Why is no one here?

He's come. He resurrected you in love.

Listen to his glorious call and drink!

His wine's for you. Ecstasy your repast.

It's a day of feasting. Drink! End your fast.

Join us on the path of unity at last!

We're one river they divided. That's passed.

Step up, man! Here's the fountain of Eden!

Friend, we'll find paradise in the hearts of men.

أدِرْ كأساً

ألا يَا سَاقِياً إنِّي، لَظَمْآنٌ وَمُشْتَاقُ

أدِرْ كأساً وَلا تُنْكِرْ، فإنَّ القَوْمَ قَدْ ذَاقُوا

إذَا مَا شِئتَ أسْرَارِي، أدِرْ كأساً مِنَ النَّارِ

فأَسْكِرْنِيْ وَسائِلِنِيْ، إلى مَنْ أنْتَ مُشْتاقُ

أضَاءَ العِشْقُ مِصبَاحاً، فصَارَ اللَّيْلُ إصبَاحاً

ومِنْ أنْوَارِهِ انشَقَّتْ عَلى الأحْجَارِ أحْداقُ

فَدَاءُ العِشْقِ آدْوائي، وَمُرُّ العِشْقِ حَلوِاني

وإنِّي بَيْنَ عُشّاقٍ، أسُوقُ حَيْثُ مَا سَاقُوا

خُذِ الدُّنْيَا وَخَلِّينَا، فَدُنْيَا العِشْقِ تَكْفينا

لَنَا في العِشْقِ جَنَّاتٌ وَبُلْدَانٌ وَأسْوَاقُ

وَأرْوَاحٌ تُلاقِينَا، وَأرْوَاحٌ سَوَاقِينَا

وخَمْرٌ فِيهِ مِدْرَارٌ، وَكَأسُ العِشْقِ رَقْرَاقُ

Fill Up My Cup!

Wine boy! I'm thirsty and full of desire.

Fill up my cup! The others had their taste.

To learn my secrets, fill me with fire.

Get me drunk. Then ask whom I admire.

My love's a lantern, turning night to dawn.

My eyes can see through stone with this love's light.

The pain of sacrifice is my elixir,

the bitterness of love my sweet delight.

I'll go with his lovers where they may roam.

So, take the world. Just leave us here alone.

Love is enough—a place where gardens grow,

with cities, shops, and loving souls we know.

They give us drink; the wine will always flow.

My cup of love sparkles with love's bright glow.

مَا كَفَرْت*

إِنَّا فَتَحْنَا عَيْنَكُمْ، فَاسْتَبْصِرُوا الغَيْبَ البَصَرْ

إِنَّا قَضَيْنَا بَيْنَكُمْ، فَاسْتَبْشِرُوا بِالمُنْتَصَرْ

إِنْ كَانَ عَيْشاً قَدْ هَجَرْ، وَاخْتَلَّ عَقْلِي مِنْ سَهَرْ

وَاللهِ رُوحِيْ مَا نَفَرْ، وَاللهِ رُوحِيْ مَا كَفَرْ

---

*ليس من المؤكد أن هذه لأبيات للرومي لأنها لا تتوافق مع طبيعة كتاباته، فهو لم يأبه بما يقوله الناس، وعبر بتواضع عن ضعفه وقناعته بأن سعادته تأتي فقط من رضى مولاه عنه. ومن الممكن أن تكون قد أدرجت في الديوان من قبل أحد أتباعه ردا على بعض التهم التي وجهت له من قبل معارضيه، منها الابتعاد عن الإسلام.

I Never Strayed*

You opened my eyes; I saw my hidden fate.

You judged me well: my victory was great!

Even dead, or mad in my sleepless state,

my soul never strayed. I was no apostate.

---

*It is doubtful that this poem is by Rumi. It could be the interpolation of some pious poet who inserted the verse into Rumi's divan to prove that he never abandoned Islam, as his critics have charged. Rumi's poems are not preachy or self-congratulatory. Quite the opposite, he often writes of his weakness and unworthiness and finds salvation only through the generosity of his master, Shams-e Trabrizi.

People of Damnation

المَغْضُوبُ عَلَيهِمْ

قَدْ رَجِعْنَا

قَدْ رَجِعْنَا، قَدْ رَجِعْنَا، جَائِباً مِنْ طُورِكُمْ

انْظُرُونَا، «انْظُرُونَا نَقْتَبِسْ مِنْ نُورِكُمْ»*

كُلُّ مَنْ يَرجُو وُجُوداً يَغْتَنِمْ مِنْ جُودِكُمْ

كُلُّ مَنْ أرداهُ عُسْرٌ نَالَ مِنْ مَيسُورِكُمْ

لَيْسَ يَشْقَى بِالرَّزَايَا مَنْ يَكُنْ مَحْفُوظَكُمْ

لا يُبَالِي بِالبَرَايَا خَاضِعِي مَنْصُورِكُمْ

حَارَتْ أبْصَارُ البَرَايَا فِي بَدِيهِيَاتِكُمْ

مَنْ يُلاقِي مَنْ يَسُوقُ الخَيْلَ فِي مَسْتُورِكُمْ

لَيْسَ يُهدي قَلْبَنا إلا نَسِيمٌ مِنْكُمْ

لَيْسَ يُجْلِي طَرْفَنَا إلا بِقُرْبَى دُورِكُمْ

---

*سورة الحديد [57] آية 13: « يَوْمَ يَقُولُ الْمُنَافِقُونَ وَالْمُنَافِقَاتُ لِلَّذِينَ آمَنُوا انظُرُونَا نَقْتَبِسْ مِنْ نُورِكُمْ قِيلَ ارْجِعُوا وَرَاءَكُمْ فَالْتَمِسُوا نُورًا فَضُرِبَ بَيْنَهُمْ بِسُورٍ لَهُ بَابٌ بَاطِنُهُ فِيهِ الرَّحْمَةُ وَظَاهِرُهُ مِنْ قِبَلِهِ الْعَذَابُ.»

Saved on Judgment Day

I came back! Came back for the love of you.

Look at me! Let me borrow some of your light.*

The ones who shall be saved know what to do:

reach out for generosity from you.

Whoever stumbles on calamity

will have your gifts, and your protection too.

No fear. I'm sheltered by your victory.

Your wisdom stuns all of humanity.

Whoever meets you will help us be free,

will lead us through your hidden mystery.

The breeze of your glance is my guide. I can't see.

No sight. My eyes know only your proximity.

---

*See Qur'an 57:13. "On that Day [of Judgment] the hypocrite men and hypocrite women will say to the true believers: 'Wait for us, that we may borrow some of your light.'"

يُحيي الصَّخْرَ

عَلَى أَهْلِ نَجْدٍ * النَّنَا وَسَلامُ

وَعَيشَتُنَا في غَيرِهِمْ لَحَرَامُ

فَضِيلَتُهُ لِلفَاضِلينَ بَصيرَةٌ

مَلاحَتُهُ لِلعَاشِقينَ قِوامُ

بَصيرَةُ أَهْلِ اللهِ مِنْهُ مُكَحَّلُ

وَعِشرَةُ أَهْلِ الحَقِّ فيهِ مُدامُ

أيا سَاكِنيها مِنْ فَضيلَةِ سَيِّدي

لَكُمْ عيشَةٌ مَرضِيَّةٌ وَدَوامُ

وَلَولا حِجَابُ العِزِّ أَرْخَى مَليكُنَا

لَكَانَ على بَابِ المَليكِ زِحَامُ

مَليكٌ إذا لاحَتْ شَعَاشِعُ خَدِّهِ

لأَصبَحَ حَيَّاً صَخرَةٌ وَرُخَامُ

سَقَى اللهُ وَقْتاً أَنْ طَغَانَا كَلامُهُ

فَفِي الرُّوحِ مِنْ ذَاكَ الكَلامِ كِلامُ

غَدَا آلِفاً قَلْبي يَقُومُ لِأمرِهِ

وَقَدِّيَ مِنْ عَذْلِ العَوَاذِلِ لامُوا

---

*نجد في الجزيرة العربية، ويرى بعض المفسرين حسب الحديث التالي أن نجد «أرض الفتن وقرن الشيطان» حيث جاء عَنِ ابْنِ عُمَرَ رضي الله عنهما قَالَ: (اللَّهُمَّ بَارِكْ لَنَا في شَأمِنَا وفي يَمَنِنَا. قَالُوا: وفي نَجْدِنَا؟ قَالَ: اللَّهُمَّ بَارِكْ لَنَا في شَأمِنَا وفي يَمَنِنَا. قَالُوا: وفي نَجْدِنَا؟ قَالَ: هُنَاكَ الزَّلازِلُ وَالفِتَنُ، وَبِهَا يَطْلُعُ قَرْنُ الشَّيْطَانِ) رواه البخاري ومسلم وهذا غير ما قاله فيها جلال الدين الرومي في هذه القصيدة.

Stones Come Alive

Peace! Praise! on the people of damnation.*

To live my life without them is a sin.

His virtues are a guide for all good men.

His beauty lights his lovers' path for them.

He sharpens the eyes of those he's chosen.

For them, your wine is fellowship with him.

The dwellers who have known my Master's giving have

found their way to paradise while living.

But for the veil of glory our king unstrung

mobs would crowd his door to do his bidding.

A king with glowing cheeks has now appeared!

The rocks, the stones wake up and they come near

to bless the day when everyone will hear

his Word. From that Word his command is clear.

He lifted up my soul. I served him here.

For that the blamers blame me, hate, and jeer.

---

*This line offers "Praise and greetings to the people of Najd." Najd is an area of Central Arabia, but some suggest it refers to an area in Iraq. This land, according to tradition, is cursed as the land of damnation. When the people of Najd asked Muhammad to pray for God's blessings on them, he refused and replied: "There will be earthquakes and afflictions there, and the horns of Satan will come out there" (Hadith from Sahih al-Bukhari, vol. 2, book 17, no. 147; vol. 9, book 88, no. 214).

لا أَخَافُ ضَلالاً

رَشَأُ العِشْقِ حَبِيبِي! لَشَرُودٌ وَمُضِلُّ
كُلُّ قَلْبٍ لِهَوَاهُ، وَجَدَ الصَّبْرَ يَصِلْ
سِنَةُ الوَصْلِ قَصِيرٌ، عَجِلٌ مُعْتَجِلّ
سِنَةُ الهَجْرِ طَوِيلٌ، وَمَدِيدٌ وَمُمِلْ
يَمْلأُ الكَأْسَ حَبِيبِي، وَطَبِيبِي وَيَذرُ
فَعِلُنْ مُفْتَعِلُنْ ، أو فَعِلاتُنْ وَفَعَلْ
نَاوَلَ الكَأْسَ نَهَاراً، وَجِهَاراً وَقِحَاً
لا يَخَافُ رَهَقاً، مَنْ بِمُحَيّاكَ قُتِلْ

I'm Not Afraid of Sin

My Lover threw his love around! I went
astray. A patient man will feel his love
that way. This patience is the kind that's short.
It rushes. It can't stay. Separation
is so long—so dull, so sad, full of dismay.

Lover! Healer! Fill up my cup. Make it
overflow. You will it, and you make it so.
You handed me your cup in broad daylight.
I died when first I saw your face. And then,
I drank your cup. I'm not afraid of sin.

أَصْحَابُ مَدْيَنٍ*

يُنَادِي الوَرْدُ يَا أَصْحَابَ مَدْيَنْ

أَلَا فَافْرِحْ بِنَا مَنْ كَانَ يَحْزَنْ

فَإِنَّ الأَرْضَ إِخْضَرَّتْ بِنُورِ

وَقَالَ اللهُ لِلعَارِيْ «تَزَيَّنْ»

وَعَادَ الهَارِبُونَ إِلَى حَيَاةٍ

وَدِيوَانُ النُّشُورِ غَدَا مُدَوَّنْ

بِأَمْرِ اللهِ مَاتُوا، ثُمَّ جَاءُوا

وَأَبْلَاهُمْ زَمَاناً، ثُمَّ أَحْسَنْ

وَشَمْسُ اللهِ طَالَعَةٌ بِفَضْلٍ

وَبُرْهَانٌ صَنَايِعُهُ مُبَرْهَنْ

وصَبَّغَنَا النَّبَاتُ بِغَيْرِ صَبْغٍ

نُقَدِّرُ حَجْمَها مِنْ غَيْرِ مَلْبَنْ

جِنَانٌ فِي جِنَانٍ فِي جِنَانٍ

أَلَا يَا حَايِراً، فِيهَا تَوَطَّنْ

وهَيَّجَنَا النُّفُوسُ إِلَى المَعَالِيْ

فَذَا نَالَ الوِصَالُ، وذَا تَفَرْعَنْ

أَلَا فَاسْكُتْ وكَلِّمْهُمْ بِصَمْتٍ

فَإِنَّ الصَّمْتَ لِلْأَسْرَارِ أَبْيَنْ

---

*مدين مكان في الجزيرة العربية جاء ذكره في سورة الأعراف [7] آية ٤٨-٥٨، ٤٩ حيث حثّ الله أهل مدين على التوبة بأن أرسل لهم نبيه شعيب ولكنّهم ما تابوا، فأرسل لهم الصيحة الكبرى التي أبادتهم، إلا القوم الصالحين.

You, People of Madyan!*

I hear the flowers shout: "Keep us alive!

We'll cheer the damned, those souls so worn and tried!"

Light dawns! The earth's now green and sanctified.

God calls to the naked, "Wear your fine robes!"

The ones who've died return now to his side.

Then he writes the Book of Resurrection!

The dead at God's command are now revived.

First, they are tested, then they learn God's grace.

The Sun† of God appears revivified,

the proof of his creation clarified.

He paints our flowers so colorfully.

Without judgment, our worth is certified.

Gardens above gardens above gardens.

You who were lost: Come! Make your home inside.

He raises every soul to ecstasy.

Some find reunion. Some are filled with pride.

Don't talk to them. Speak to them in silence.

The best teacher of secrets is silence.

---

*Madyan was a city in Arabia condemned in the Qur'an in sura 7. See verses 84, 85, and 95. God called on the people of Madyan through his prophet Shuaib to repent, and when they did not, they were destroyed by earthquakes and thunderbolts.
†The "Sun" refers to shams, that is, Shams-e Tabrizi.

سِرْ إلى تَبْرِيزَ

مَرَرْتُ بِدُرٍّ في هَواهُ بِحَارُ

رَأوْهُ بُدُوراً في الدَّلالِ وَحارُوا

وَشاهَدْتُ ماءً شابَهَ الرُّوحَ في الصَّفا

ويَعشَقُ ذاكَ الماءَ ما هُوَ نَارُ

وَللعِشْقِ نُورٌ لَيْسَ للشّمسِ مِثلهُ

فَظَلَّ دَليلَ العَاشِقينَ وَسارُوا

عَرُوسُ الهَوى بَدرٌ تَلأْلأَ في الدُّجى

عليها دِماءُ العَاشِقينَ خِمارُ

ظَلِلْتُ مِنَ الدُّنيا على طَلَبِ الهَوى

أَضاءَ لَنا غَيرَ الدِّيارِ دِيارُ

فَشاهَدْتُ رُكبَاناً قَريحاً مَطِيُّهُمْ

وَكانَ لَهُمْ عِنْدَ المَسيرِ بِدَارُ

فَقُلتُ لَهُمْ في ذَاكَ، قَالوا لَفَيْ الهَوى

لِمَنْ فَرَّ مِنَ هَذي الدِّيارِ دَمَارُ

وَإنْ شِئتَ بُرْهَاناً فَسَافِرْ بِبَلَدةٍ

يُقالُ لَها تَبريزُ* وَهْيَ مَزَارُ

فَيَشتَمُّ أَهْلُ العِشْقِ مِن تُرْبَاتِه

وَللرُّوحِ مِنها زُخْرُفٌ وَسِوَارُ

تَروحُ كَلَيْلٍ مُظْلِمٍ في هَوائِه

وتَرجِعُ مَسرُوراً وَأنتَ نَهَارُ

---

*مدينة شمس الدين التبريزي.

Walk to Tabriz

For love, I passed up jewels. I crossed the sea.

The full moon flickered in perplexity.

Water, pure as a sinless soul, I see.

The ones on fire love its purity.

His love shines brighter than the sun. So free!

It guides lovers on their sacred journey.

Just like a bride of love, he lights a dark

country, veiled with the blood of his lovers.

Lost, I went in search of his charity.

He had lit up so many homes. Not mine.

I saw the wounded riding past. They pushed

their horses on and left us all behind.

I asked them why they did that. They replied:

"Love leaves all in destruction, you will find.

We flee. If you need proof, then walk to a

city called Tabriz,* a holy place to stay.

From its dust, lovers breathe his fragrant scent.

With jewels, they dress their souls just as they may."

With gloomy heart, I came looking for love.

I found him—and his light brightened my day.

---

*Rumi's master, Shams-e Tabrizi, came from Tabriz.

The Victory

الفَوزُ

الرَّبِيعُ الإلَهِي

جَاءَ الرَّبِيعُ وَالبَطَرْ، زَالَ الشِّتَاءُ والخَطَرْ

مِنْ فَضْلِ رَبٍّ عِنْدَهُ، كُلُّ الخَطَايا تُغْتَفَرْ

أوحَى إِليْكُمْ رَبُّكُمْ، أَنَّا غَفَرْنَا ذَنْبَكُمْ

وَارْضَوْا بِما يُقْضَى لَكُمْ، إِنَّ الرِّضَا خَيْرُ السِّيَرْ

وَقَائِلٍ يَقُولُ لِي: إِنَّا عَلِمْنا بِرَّهُ

فَاخْكِ لَدَيْنا سِرَّهُ، لا تَشْتَغِلْ فِيما اشْتَهَرْ

السِّرُّ فِيكَ يا فَتَى، لا تَلْتَمِسْ فِيما أَتَى

مَنْ لَيْسَ سِرٌّ عِنْدَهُ، لَمْ يَنْتَفِعْ مِمَّا ظَهَرْ

انْظُرْ إِلى أَهْلِ الرَّدَى، كَمْ عَايَنُوا نُورَ الهُدَى

لَمْ تَرْتَفِعْ أَسْتَارُهُمْ، مِنْ بَعْدِ ما انشَقَّ القَمَرْ

يا رَبَّنا رُبَّ المِنَنْ، إِنْ أَنْتَ لَمْ تَرْحَمْ، فَمَنْ؟

مِنْكَ الهُدَى، مِنْكَ الرَّدَى، مَا غَيْرُ ذَا إِلا غَرَرْ

يا شَوْقُ أَيْنَ العَافِيَةْ، كَيْ أظْطَفِرْ بالقَافِيَةْ؟

عِنْدِي صِفَاتٌ صَافِيَةْ، فِي جَنْبِها نُطْقِي كَدَرْ

إِنْ كَانَ نُطْقِي مُدْرِسِي، قَدْ ظَلَّ عِشْقِي مُخرِسِي

وَالعِشْقُ قِرْنٌ غَالِبٌ فِينَا وسُلطَانُ الظَّفَرْ

سِرٌّ كَتِيمٌ لَفْظُهُ، سَيْفٌ حَسِيمٌ لَحْظُهُ

شَمْسُ الضُّحَى لا تَخْتَفِي، إِلّا بِسَحَّارٍ سَحَرْ

يا سَاحِراً أَبْصَارَنَا، بَالَغْتَ فِي أسْحَارِنَا

فَارْفُقْ بِنَا أو دَارِنا، إِنَّا حُبِسْنا فِي السَّفَرْ

يا قَوْمَ مُوسَى إِنَّا، فِي التِّيهِ تِهْنَا مِثلَكُمْ

كَيْفَ اهتَدَيْتُمْ فاخْبِرُوا، لا تَكْتُمُوا عَنَّا الخَبَرْ

Divine Springtime

Spring is here, full of promises. The threat

of winter melts, and God forgives our sins.

He said it: "I have canceled every debt."

Smile! Take your portion. This is the best step.

One shouts: "We've heard about his mercy! So, let

us know his secrets, not this common talk!"

The secret is inside you, man. Don't fret.

Who doesn't find that secret will regret

he's lost the prize. Look! The damned see his light,

but veil their eyes until Moon has set.

Lord of Mercy! If you show no mercy,

who will have mercy then? You are life, yet

you are death—all else is false, just regret.

My Desire! Give me strength. Let these rhymes come.

My thoughts are pure, but my words come undone.

Speech is my teacher, but love strikes me dumb.

Love was our great victory! A secret

never spoken: a sword with a sharp blade.

The sun can't dim, unless a great magician

casts his spell. And a mighty spell you made!

Lord! Have mercy! I am in prison here.

Tribe of Moses! Like you, I am vanity.

إِنْ عَوَّقُوا تِرْحَالَنَا، فَالمَنُّ والسَّلْوَى لَنَا

أَصْلَحْتَ رَبِّي بَالَنَا، طَابَ السَّفَرْ، طَابَ الْحَضَرْ

اسْكُتْ وَلَا تُكْثِرْ أَخِي، إِنْ طَلْتَ تُكْثِرْ تَرتَخِي

الْحَبْلُ فِي رِيحِ الْهَوَى، فَاحْفَظْهُ «كَلَّا لَا وَزَرْ»*

إِنَّ الْهَوَى قَدْ غَرَّنَا، مِنْ بَعْدِ مَا قَدْ سَرَّنَا

فَاكْشِفْ بِلُطْفٍ ضُرَّنَا، قَالَ النَّبِيُّ: «لَا ضَرَرْ»†

قَالُوا: «نُدَبِّرْ شَأْنَكُمْ، نَفْتَحْ لَكُمْ آذَانَكُمْ

نَرْفَعْ لَكُمْ أَرْكَانَكُمْ، أَنْتُمْ مَصَابِيحْ البَشَرْ»

«ز اندازه بيرون خورده ام، كاندازه را گم كرده ام»‡

شُدُّوا يَدِي، شُدُّوا فَمِي، هَذَا دَوَاءُ مَنْ سَكِرْ

هَاكُمْ مَعَارِيجَ اللِّقَا، فِيهَا تَدَارِيجُ البَقَا

أَنْعِمْ بِهِ مِنْ مُسْتَقَى، أَكْرِمْ بِهِ مِنْ مُسْتَقَرْ

العَيْشُ حَقًّا عَيْشُكُمْ، والمَوْتُ حَقًّا مَوتُكُمْ

والدِّينُ والدُّنْيَا لَكُمْ، هَذَا جَزَاءُ مَنْ شَكَرْ

---

* سورة القيامة [57] آية 10-11: تشرح السورة حال البشر يوم القيامة بما فيها، «يَقُولُ الْإِنْسَانُ يَوْمَئِذٍ أَيْنَ الْمَفَرُّ. كَلَّا لَا وَزَرَ.»

†أصل الحديث: «لا ضرر ولا ضرار» (الجامع الصغير، طبعة مصر، دار الكتب العربية الكبرى ج٢، ص ٢٠٢). ويعني نفي الضرر فيما شرعه الله لعباده من الأحكام، ونهي المؤمنين عن إحداث الضرر أو فعله.

‡من الفارسية وترجمته: شربت إلى ما بعد الحدود، حتى أضعت فهمي للحدود.

Who guided you? Just tell me. Let me hear.

I'm jailed, but I dine on quail and manna.

My journey's good, and my confinement dear.

Hush, my brothers! No need to beg for grace.

That rope in the storm of passion, hide it!

But I know well it has no hiding place.*

I lost my passion. Once it gave me joy.

No harm. The Prophet says there's no disgrace.†

He said: "I'll care for you. You'll hear me speak.

I'll raise you up to be a guiding light!"

I'm drunk. No limits—and none do I seek.‡

So, tie my hands and close my mouth,

for that's the only cure, for those who reek.

That was the height of reunion, the goal.

A sacred house! A wellspring for the soul!

True living is your life, true dying your death.

Faith and life upon those who are thankful.

---

*Qur'an 75:10–11: "Man will say on that Day, 'Where is the [place of] escape?' No! There is no refuge."

†This line is based on an Islamic hadith that states that there is should be "no harm and no reciprocated harm" from implementing God's Laws (*Aljami al-Saghir* [Egypt: Dar al-Kutub al-Arabiah al-Kubra], 2:202).

‡This verse is the translation of a line in Persian.

تَوَطَّن فِيَّ

أَيَا بَدْرَ الدُّجَى، بَلْ أَنْتَ أَحْسَنْ
إِذَا وَافَاكَ قَلْبٌ، كَيْفَ يَحْزَنْ؟

فَصِرْ يَا قَلْبُ فِي سُوقِ المَعَالِيْ
لَهُ رَهْناً، إِذا مَا كُنْتَ تُرْهَنْ

أَيَا نَجْماً خَنُوساً فِي ذُرَاهُ
تَكَنَّسْ فِي صُعُودِكَ أَوْ تَوَطَّنْ

فَلا يَعْلُوكَ نَحْسٌ أَنْتَ آمِنْ
وَلا يَغْشَاكَ فَقْرٌ أَنْتَ مَخْزَنْ

أَيَا جِسْماً فَنَيْتَ فِي هَوَاهُ
لَهُ عُذْرٌ وَبُرْهَانٌ مُبَرْهَنْ

وَأَرْضِعْنِي لِبَاناً تَرْتَضِيهِ
فَمَنْ أَرْضَعْتَهُ فَهُوَ المُسَمَّنْ

إِذَا مَا لَمْ يَذُقْهُ كَيْفَ يَحْيَا؟
وَإِنَّ الخُلْدَ يَدْخُلُهُ مَنْ آمَنْ

Make Your Home Mine

In the dark of blackest night, you are moonlight

and more beautiful! How can I be sad?

If I could buy you back, my soul—tonight

I'd sell for cash on heaven's auction block.

I am but a dim shadow in his light.

My home is with him—swept up in his flight.

No harm can befall me in your heaven.

No want can ever steal my full birthright.

My life spent in worship at your temple—

that's my excuse! You are my second sight.

I will drink the milk that you find worthy.

I will get fat on the breast of your might.

The babe who does not suckle cannot live.

Only those with faith find eternal light.

اللامَكَانُ

أطْيَبُ الأسْفَارِ عِنْدِي، انْتِقَالِيْ مِنَ مَكَانْ

فَالمَكَانَاتُ حِجَابٌ عَنْ عَيَانِ اللامَكَانْ

المَكَانَاتُ خَوَابِي، لا مَكَانَ بَحْرُ الفُرَاتْ*

يُنْتِنُ المَاءَ الزُّلالَ طُولُ حَبْسٍ في الجِنَانِ

في البَيَانِ انْفِرَاجٌ في مَطَارٍ لِلضَّمِيرِ

يا ضَمِيرِي طِرْ سِرَاراً، لا تَطِرْ صَوبَ البَيَانِ

انْتِقَالٌ لِلدَّجَاجِ وَسْطَ دَارٍ لِلحُبُوبِ

وَانْتِقَالٌ لِلطُّيُورِ فَوْقَ جَوٍّ لِلأَمَانِ

يا فَتى شَتَّانَ بَيْنَ انْتِقَالٍ وَانْتِقَالِ

انْتِقَالٍ في هَوَانٍ وَانْتِقَالٍ في جِنَانِ

في كِلا النَّقْلَيْنِ ذَوْقٌ في ابْتِدَاءِ الانْتِهَاضِ

إنَّمَا الفَرْقُ سَيَبْدُوا آخِراً لِلافْتِتَانِ

---

*نهر الفرات، أطول نهر في شرق آسيا، ويشكل مع نهر دجلة أهم معالم العراق.

No Place

The best beloved of all things in my sight

is to leave one place for another place.

Place is a blindfold to seeing no-place.

Place is a jar. The river* flows past place.

Pure water grows stagnant in a garden.

Beautiful words may open the mind's place.

But, my soul! Fly free! Not to some word's place.

Baby chicks scramble in a room full of grain—

a flock of birds flies toward the horizon.

Man, each one is a very different game.

One brings shame. The other is paradise.

Both will gain. Both are movement on a plane.

But see the difference: one of them is Love.

---

*The river referred to in this line is the Euphrates, the longest river in Western Asia. The Euphrates and the Tigris are the two defining rivers of Mesopotamia.

النُّورُ الإلَهِي

جُوْدُ الشُّمُوسِ عَلَى الوَرَى إشْرَاقُ
وَوَرَاءَها نُورُ الهَوَى بَرَّاقُ

وَوَرَاءَ أنْوَارِ الهَوَى لِي سَيِّدٌ
ضَاءَتْ لَنَا بِضِيَائِهِ الآفَاقُ

مَا أطْيَبَ العُشَّاقَ فِي أشوَاقِهِمْ
العِشْقُ أيْضاً نَحْوَهُمْ مُشتَاقُ

هَمُّوا لِرُؤْيَتِهِ فَلَاحَتْ شَمْسُهُ
حَارَتْ وَكَلَّتْ نَحْوَهُ الأحْدَاقُ

نَادَى مُنَادٍ عَاشِقِيهِ بِدَعْوَةٍ
طَفِقُوا إلى صَوْتِ النِّدَاءِ وَسَاقُوا

سَكِرُوا بِرُؤْيَتِهِ وَرَاحِ لِقَائِهِ
لا تَحْسَبُوهُمْ بَعْدَ ذَاكَ أفَاقُوا

إنْ شِئتَ مَنْ يَحْكِيكَ بَرْقَ خُدُودِهِ
ضَعْفِيْ وَصُفْرَةُ وَجْنَتِي مِصْدَاقُ

Divine Light

The Sun shines rays of light with generosity.

Behind this light is love and luminosity.

Behind that glow of love stands my Master.

He lights the horizon in its immensity.

His lovers pine on for their day of unity.

His love is waiting—longing for them too.

They walked toward him. His sun rose with ferocity.

Their eyes went blind from its stunning intensity.

Then he called them all to be his lovers.

They rushed to him, led others to his company.

They got drunk on the wine of his intimacy,

and they never woke up sober again.

Do you want more proof of his light's infinity?

My weak limbs, my blood-drained face are testimony.

أغْنِيةُ اللّيْلِ

حَدَا البَشِيرُ بِشَارَةً يَا جَارُ

دَهِشَ الفُؤَادُ بِمَا حَدَاهُ وَحَارُوا

سَمِعُوا نِداءَ الحَقِّ مِنْ فَمِ طَارِقٍ

قَرُبَ الخِيامُ إِلَيْكُمُ وَالدَّارُ

وَدَنَا كَرِيمٌ وَجْهُهُ قَمَرُ الدُّجَى

وَخَيَالُهُ لِلْعَاشِقِينَ مَدَارُ

فَتَحَلَّقُوا حَوْلَ البَشِيرِ وَأَقْبَلُوا

سَجَدُوا جَمِيعاً لِلْبَشِيرِ وَزَارُوا

سَكَنَتْ قُلُوبٌ بَعْدَ مَا سَكَنَ البَلا

لَبِسُوا لِباسَ الجَدِّ مِنْهُ وَسَارُوا

Night Song

Listen, My Friends!

Last night he sang his glad tidings so near.

I was stunned by his song, my heart in fear.

I heard the call of God from his caller.

He even passed among us, came right here!

So Generous!

So close! His face the moon on a dark night—

even his shadow a sign of his might—

and that is where his lovers turned to pray.

Those lovers circled round. They came to stay.

Glad tidings!

They all bowed down, prostrate in certainty,

and this became their sacred pilgrimage.

I calmed my heart after that great calamity,

walked on wearing the cloth of his bounty.

العِشْقُ

فَدَيْتُ سَيِّدَنَا أَنَّهُ يَرَى وَيَجُودُ

إِلى البَقَاءِ يُبَلِّغُ مِنَ الفَنَاءِ يَذُودُ

مَعَاذُ كُلِّ شُرُودٍ طَغَى وَمِنْهُ نَأَى

مِثَالُ ظِلِّكَ إِنْ طَالَ هُوَ إِلَيْكَ يَعُودُ

بِأَمْرِ حَافِظَةِ اللهِ المَكَانَ يَعِي

بِمَسِّ عَاطِفَةِ اللهِ الزَّمَانُ وَلُودُ

أَيَا فُؤَادَ قَدُبْ فِي لَظَى مَحَبَّتِهِ

أَيَا حَيَاةَ فَدُومِي فَقَدْ أَتَاكِ خُلُودُ

تُرِيدُ جَبْرَ جَبِيرٍ الفُؤَادِ فَانْكَسِرَنْ

تُرِيدُ نِحْلَةَ تَاجٍ فَلا تَنِي بِسُجُودُ

بِرَغْمِ أَنْفِكَ لا تَنْكَسِرْ كَمَا الحَيَوانُ

بِنِصْفِ وَجْهِكَ لا تَسْجُدَنْ شَبِيهَ يَهُودْ*

يَقُولُ لَيْتَ حَبِيبِي يُحِبُّنِي كَرَماً

أَلَيْسَ حُبُّكَ تَأْثِيرُ حُبِّ وُدٍّ وَدُودْ؟

أَيَا نَضَاةَ عَيْشِي، بِما تُهَيِّجُنِي

مَتَى تَقَرُّ عُيُونِي وَصَاحِبِي مَفْقُودْ؟

لَئِنْ سَكِرْتَ بِمَا قَدْ سَقَيْتَنِي يَا دَهْرُ

أَكُونُ مِثْلَكَ لُدّاً «لِرَبِّهِ لَكَنُودْ»†

Passion

I give my life to you, who gives me breath,

Master of salvation, who conquers death,

resurrected in each moment fleeing by.

Like your shadow, if I stray with desire,

I know I always come back to your feet.

God's Secret! Space finds new life you inspire.

Mercy of God! Your touch makes time complete.

My heart is melting in my lover's fire,

and so my life will never taste defeat.

If you want to mend your heart, break it more!

Want a crown? Raise your forehead off the floor!

Don't thrash against your will like some wild boar.

Don't offer two-faced prayers like some traitor.*

You want your Master's gifts of love once more?

Love will start when the loved one's passions soar.

He gives me life, brings me restless longing!

I'll never rest without my lover near.

If I delight in this life's dull reward,

then I have been ungrateful to my Lord.†

---

*This line refers to the Jews of Medina, who broke their treaty promises to Muhammad and turned against him.

†Qur'an 100:6, "Indeed mankind, to his Lord, is ungrateful."

نِهَايَةُ الحُزْنِ

تَعَالَ يَا مَدَدَ العَيْشِ وَالسُّرُورِ تَعَالْ
تَعَالَ يَا فَرَجَ الهَمّ فَاتِحَ الأَقْفَالْ
لِقَاءُ وَجْهِكَ في الهَمّ فَالِقُ الإِصْبَاحِ
سِقَاءُ جُودِكَ في الفَقْرِ مُنْتَهَى الإِقْبَالْ
تَعَالَ إِنَّكَ عِيسَى فَأَحْيِ مَوْتَانَا
تَعَالَ وَادْفَعْ عَنَّا خَدِيعَةَ الدَّجَّالْ
تَعَالَ إِنَّكَ دَاوُدُ فَاتَّخِذْ زَرَداً
تَصُونُ مُهْجَتَنَا مِنْ إِصَابَةِ الأَنْصَالْ
تَعَالَ إِنَّكَ مُوسَى تَشُقُّ بَحْرَ رَدَى
لِكَيْ تُغَرِّقَ فِرْعَونَ، سَيِّءَ الأَفْعَالْ
تَعَالَ أَنْتَ نُوحٌ وَنَحْنُ في الطُّوفَانِ
أَما سَفِينَةُ نُوحٍ تُعَدُّ لِلأَهْوَالْ؟
فَهُمْ صِفَاتُكَ لَكِنْ تَصَوَّرَتْ بَشَراً
فَكَمْ لِفَضْلِكَ أَمْثَالَهُمْ بِلا أَمْثَالْ
يُحِيلُ طَالِبُ دُنْيا وُجُودَكَ الأَعْلَى
وَفي وُجُودِكَ دُنْيَاهُ بَاطِلٌ وَمُحَالْ

End My Sadness

Come! Giver of my life and happiness.

Come! End my sadness. Open wide the door.

In times of grief, your face brings up the dawn.

You offer gifts, so I am never poor.

Come! You are Jesus Christ, so raise the dead!

Protect me from the Devil's lies once more.

Come! You are King David! Take up your sword.

Save my heart from raised daggers of discord.

Come! You are Moses. Part the deadly sea,

then drown the Pharaoh and his evil ways.

Come! You are Noah. The flood is rising.

Your ark is ready for these terrible days.

You are one man, yet are all this I praise!

Unique! Generous! You always amaze.

Before your face, the world sees it has erred.

Yes, at your feet, the world becomes absurd.

نَصْرُ اللهِ

جَاءَ نَصْرُ اللهِ حَقّاً مُسْتَجِيباً دَاعِيَا
أنْ تَعَالَوا يَا كِرَامي، وَادْخُلُوا بَيْنَ الكِرَامِ
قَالَ: «إنَّ اللهَ يَدْعُوا، اخْرُجُوا مِن ضِيقِكُمْ
إنَّ عُقْبَى مُلْتَقَانَا، مَشعَرُ البَيْتِ الحَرَامِ»
إن تَكُنْ إسْماً، فَإسْمٌ بالمُسَمَّى مَازِجٌ
لا كَإسْمٍ شِبْهَ غِمْدٍ وَالمُسَمَّى كَالحُسَامِ

The Victory

The victory of God is here!

The Day that we all craved.

Gather, friends! Walk in with the saved.

He is calling. Forget your cares.

He is Mecca! No one compares.

If he has a name, his name is one.

Not some false name that's just a shield

to hide a sword that's come undone.

لَنْ يُغْنِيكَ الذَّهَبُ

يا مُكْثِرَ الدَّلالِ عَلَى الخَلْقِ بِالنُّشُوز

الفَوْزُ فِي لِقَائِكَ، طُوبَى لِمَنْ يَفُوز

إِنْ لَمْ يَكُنْ لِقَلْبِكَ فِي ذَاتِهِ غِنَىّ

لَم تُغْنِهِ المَناصِبُ وَالمَالُ وَالكُنُوز

إِنْ كُنْتَ ذَا غِنىّ وَغِناكَ مُكَتَّمّ

كَمْ حَبَةٍ مُكَتَّمَةٍ تَرْصُدُ البُرُوز

يَا طَالِبَ الجَواهِرِ فَالدُّرُّ وَالحَصى

مِثْلانِ فِي الظَّلامِ فَهَلْ تَدْري ما تَحُوز؟

اسْتَمْحِنِ النُّقُودَ بِمِيزَانٍ صَادِقٍ

رَدّاً لِمَا يَضُرُّكَ، مَدّاً لِمَا يَعُوز

You Can't Find Wealth in Gold

You generous caller! Who call people and guide,

salvation's found just standing by your side.

Not satisfied with riches in your heart?

You can't find wealth in gold and jewels outside.

If you have riches, but those are things you hide.

They are like seeds that you have kept inside.

You ask for jewels, gems, and pretty pebbles.

In darkness, they will all look just the same.

In darkness, you can't even count your gain.

Use your wealth in some way that is humane:

Protect yourself from life's adversity.

Be generous in your prosperity.

لا تَهْدِمُوا دَارِيْنِكُمْ *

رُحْتُ أَنَا مِنْ بِيْنِكُمْ، غِبْتُ كَذَا مِنْ عَيْنِكُمْ

لا تَغْفُلُوا عَنْ حِيْنِكُمْ، لا تَهْدِمُوا دَارِيْنِكُمْ

إِخْوَانَنَا! إِخْوَانَنَا! إِنَّ الزَّمَانَ خَانَنَا

لا تَنسَأوا هِجْرَانَنَا، لا تَهْدِمُوا دَارِيْنِكُمْ

قَدْ فَاتَنَا أَعْمَارُنَا، وَاسْتُنْسِيَتْ أَخْبَارُنَا

واسْتُثْقِلَتْ أَوْزَارُنَا، لا تَهْدِمُوا دَارِيْنِكُمْ

اسْتَوثِقُوا أَدْيَانَكُمْ، وَاسْتَغْنِمُوا إِخْوَانَكُمْ

وَاسْتَعْشِقُوا إِيْمَانَكُمْ، لا تَهْدِمُوا دَارِيْنِكُمْ

---

*مع أن هذه الأبيات أدرجت في الديوان، إلا أننا غير واثقين من أنها من أبيات الرومي لاختلافها مع طرحه وفلسفته، حيث جاءت واعظة مليئة بالفخر على خلاف أسلوب الرومي وفحوى أعماله.

Don't Destroy Your Homes*

Brothers, I left you. Now I'm out of sight.

Don't forget your destiny—those two homes.

One's here, one's made of light. Don't destroy them.

Brothers! Brothers! Time was our enemy.

Don't forget me. Don't destroy both your homes.

I wasted my life. I'm forgotten now.

I was such a burden. Save both your homes.

Build up your faith. Hold fast to your brothers!

Fall in love with Truth. Don't destroy both homes.

• 89

---

*Preachy and self-righteous, it is doubtful that this poem is by Rumi, although it is included in his divan.

رَاجِعُون

نَحْنُ إلى سَيِّدِنا رَاجِعُون
طَيِّبَةَ النَّفْسِ بِهِ طَايِعُون
سَيِّدُنَا يُصبِحُ يَبْتَاعُنَا
أنفُسَنا نَحْنُ لَهُ بَايِعُون
يُفسِدُ إنْ جَاعَ إلى مَأكَلٍ
نَحْنُ إلى نَظرَتِهِ جَايِعُون
سَوْفَ تُلاقِيهِ بِمِيعَادِهِ
تَحْسَبُ أنَّا أبَداً ضَايِعُون؟

Returning

Soon, I'll be returning to my Master,

and soon I will obey his kind command.

He'll buy me in the morning when he wakes,

and I will sell myself at his demand.

The hungry man devours his first meal.

I'm starving for his glance, you understand?

I will find him. Soon we'll be together.

Did you think I'd be lost down here forever?

APPENDIX

The Arabic poems in this book are taken from volumes two, three, and four of *Kulliyat Shams ya Divan-e kabir*, edited by Badi-u-Zaman Furuzanfar (Tehran: Amir Kabir Press, 1957). They have been lightly edited by Nesreen Akhtarkhavari and Aref Awad al-Helal to correct diacritical marks, word endings, and spellings, and to preserve the integrity of the poems' meter. The corresponding numbers of each of the poems and lines in Furuzanfar's book are listed below. For example, "(1011: 1066, 10666–10667)" refers to poem number 1011, line 1066 and lines 10666 through 10667.

You Are Beautiful!

"The Glance" (894: 9364–9365)

"You Are Beautiful!" (1011: 1066, 10666–10667)

"Eastern Star" (1008: 10643–10648)

"Kill Me Now" (2121: 22443–22446, 22455–22456)

"I Can't Wait" (1783: 18660–18666)

"Mirage" (1012: 1069, 10671, 10673, 10675, 10677, 10682)

"I Lost My Mind" (1365: 14435–14443)

"I Almost Lost My Faith" (1267: 13416–13417)

"Rescue Me!" (1368: 14452–14450)

The Agony of Love

"Love's Secret" (1412: 14945, 14947)

"The Agony of Love" (2273: 2412–24128)

"You Are the Sun!" (1176: 12525–12530)

"There Will Be Blood" (1014: 10702–10708)

"You're Empty" (1782: 18656–18659)

"Put on Your Jewels" (2123: 122466–122483)

"The Path of Love" (2126: 22487–22494)

"Love and Pain" (2268: 24088–24096)
"My Heart Melts" (2127: 22495–22500)
"Come to the Light" (1346: 14422–14428, 14433–14434)

Wine of Reunion

"Sacred Wine" (2122: 22463–22465)
"Wine of Reunion" (660: 6878, 6884, 6890, 6896, 6904)
"He Resurrected You" (1780: 18644–18650)
"Fill Up My Cup!" (2249: 2497–24102)
"I Never Strayed" (1016: 10714, 10722)

People of Damnation

"Saved on Judgment Day" (1781: 18651–18655)
"Stones Come Alive" (1784: 18667–18674)
"I'm Not Afraid of Sin" (1367: 14448–14451)
"You, People of Madyan!" (2120: 22430–22438)
"Walk to Tabriz" (2274: 24129–24138)

The Victory

"Divine Springtime" (1172: 12448, 12450, 12452, 12452, 12456, 12458, 12460,
    12462, 12464, 12466, 12468, 12470, 12472, 12474, 12476, 12478, 12480)
"Make Your Home Mine" (2124: 22469–22480)
"No Place" (2125: 22481–22486)
"Divine Light" (2271: 24109–24115)
"Night Song" (2272: 24116–24120)
"Passion" (1013: 10684, 10686, 10688, 10690, 10692, 10694, 10696, 10698,
    10700)
"End My Sadness" (1369: 14457–14464)
"The Victory" (1583: 16599–16600, 16603)
"You Can't Find Wealth in Gold" (1199: 12752, 12765–12767, 12769)
"Don't Destroy Your Homes" (1778: 8635–8638)
"Returning" (2129: 22519–22522)